BASHII (THWACK)

SFX: GA (TOK) GA GA

GYA (SKWIK)

D0067852

GO
(GROK)

ARMOR: KAWAZOE

ARMOR: KAWAZOE

BAMBOO BLADE
バンブーブレード

BAMBOO BLADE 1 CONTENTS

Chapter ①:
A Girl and Her Broom ····· 3

Chapter ②:
New Members and the Ping-Pong Club ····· 29

Chapter ③:
Kojiro and the Most Valuable Thing ····· 55

Chapter ④:
Toyama and Iwasa ····· 71

Chapter ⑤:
Toyama and His Shoes ····· 97

Chapter ⑥:
Toyama and the Carbon Shinai ····· 113

Chapter ⑦:
Toyama and His Pride ····· 135

Chapter ⑧:
Tamaki and Blade Braver ····· 155

Chapter ⑨:
Kojiro and the Day He Gave Up the Shinai of His Heart ····· 177

Chapter ⑩:
Kojiro and Bento ····· 197

Story: Masahiro Totsuka / Art: Aguri Igarashi

THAT'S ENOUGH, TAMAKI. GOOD WORK.
YOU HAVE STUDIES TO ATTEND TO.

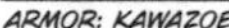
ARMOR: KAWAZOE

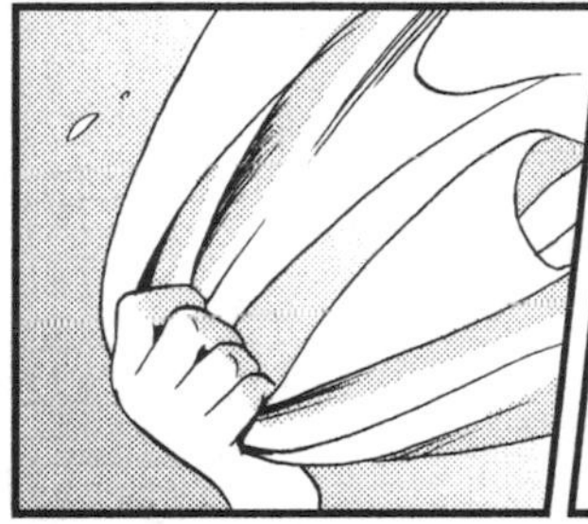

NOT EVEN A DROP OF SWEAT...

WANNA MAKE A BET?

THESE WORDS STARTED IT ALL.

SOUNDS GOOD TO ME!!

I'LL TAKE THAT BET! I'D BE CRAZY NOT TO!

GAAAA (VRMMMMMM)

GAA (GRNN)

I'M GONNA GET FIVE WARRIORS TOGETHER!
AND IT'S GONNA BE THE BEST DAMN ARMY YOU EVER SAW!
I'M BEGGING YOU!
HAA
HAA
YOU GOTTA JOIN... YOU JUST GOTTA!
I NEED YOUR HELP!!

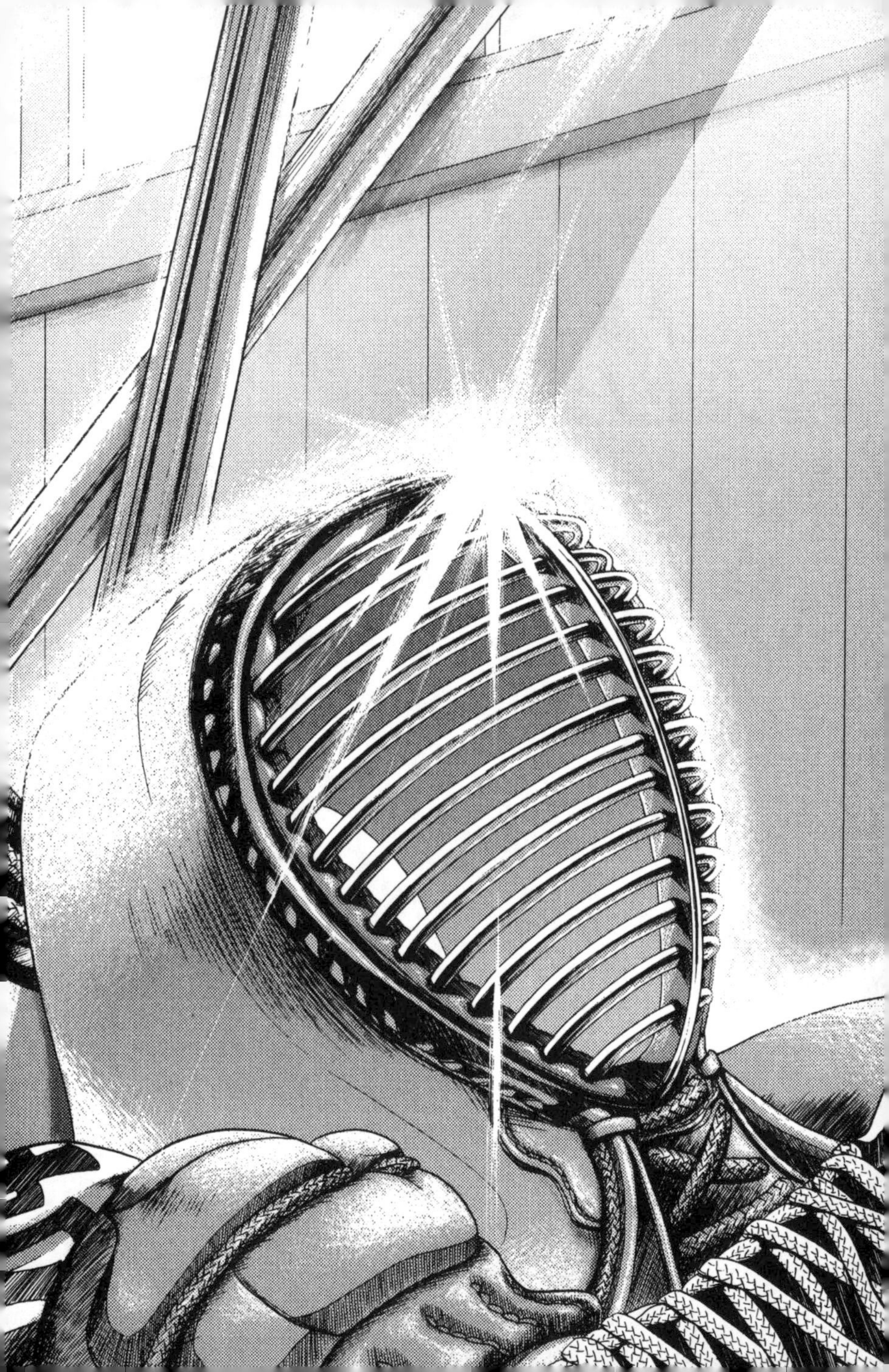

CHAPTER 1
A GIRL AND HER BROOM

TWO DAYS AGO.
SIGN: MUROE PRIVATE SENIOR HIGH SCHOOL
私立室江高等学校
SIGN: KENDO CLUB
剣道部
TONIGHT? I DUNNO...
...I DOUBT I'LL HAVE THE TIME TO MAKE IT OUT, SENPAI...

SFX: BUIN (SWISH) BUIN

ARMOR: CHIBA

COME ON, KOJIRO-SENSEI! YOU'RE THE TEAM ADVISOR!
ALL THE THIRD-YEARS ARE BUSY STUDYING FOR ENTRANCE EXAMS!
WE'VE GOT TO SHOOT FOR THE STARS FOR THEM!
優勝
UKKYAA (WOOHOO)
BUT ALL THE SECOND-YEARS ARE NO-SHOWS ASIDE FROM YOU.
FLAG: VICTORY ARMOR: MUROE HIGH / CHIBA
千葉
JUST WAIT UNTIL WE GET SOME NEW MEMBERS.
THERE'S NO USE TRYING WITH YOU ALONE.
BOOO!
GARAAN (ECHOOO)
COME ON, SENSEI! SPAR WITH ME!
I'M TOO HUNGRY TO BE JUMPING AROUND.
MAN UP!! YOU'RE A TEACHER!!
GUUUU (GROWL)
TAKE IT EASY. IT'S JUST A CLUB.

C'MON, SENSEI! HELP ME IMPROVE MY SWING!

ぴし PISHI (FWAP)

OW-OW-OW!! I DON'T HAVE ANY GUARDS ON!!

ぴし PISHI

YOU'RE JUST HITTING ME BECAUSE YOU WANT TO!

I'VE GOT...NO MONEY...

NOT EVEN A LITTLE... LITERALLY, NONE...

I'LL JUST HAVE TO CUT DOWN ON MY FOOD BUDGET.
THOSE INSTANT NOODLE CUPS ARE ACTUALLY EXPENSIVE... GOTTA RATION 'EM.

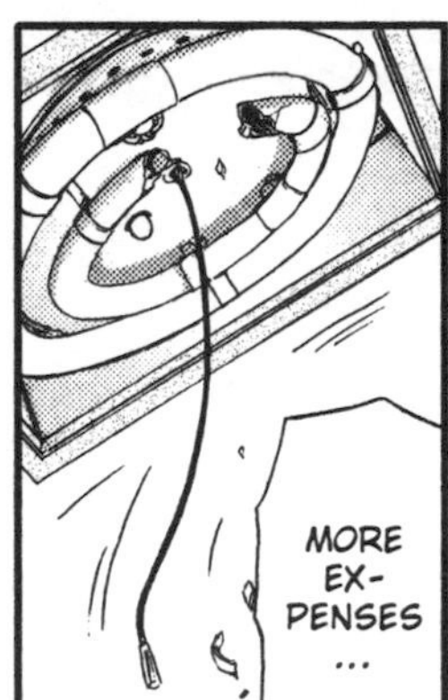

TO BE HONEST, I HAD ENOUGH TROUBLE HANDLING MY OWN PROBLEMS WITHOUT GETTING INVOLVED WITH MY STUDENTS'.

THIS IS PATHETIC...

I WAS MORE EXCITED ABOUT MY PAYCHECK THAN ABOUT ANY NEW MEMBERS.

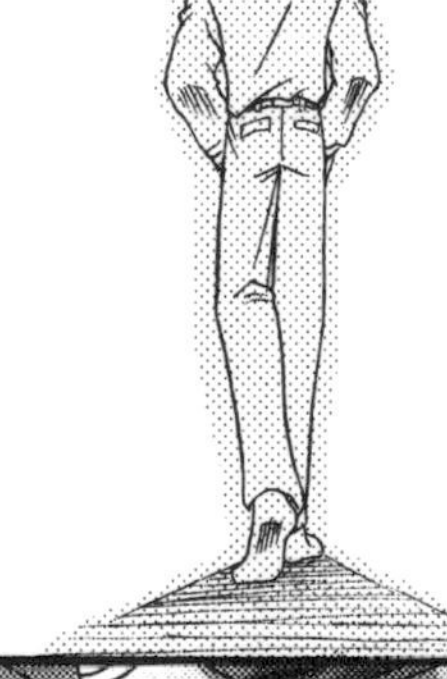

SIGNS: YAKITORI - NEKOHACHI

BUT THIS WAS THE DAY WHEN EVERYTHING CHANGED, AND I WAS REBORN.

焼き鳥

ISN'T IT HARD TRYING TO WORK TWO SCHOOLS AT ONCE, SENPAI?
YOU GOT IT!

AND THAT'S WHAT MAKES ME SO GREAT— I CAN PULL IT OFF!
わはは
WA-HA-HA!
ドヤドヤ

SFX: DOYA (YAMMER) DOYA

YOU'VE ALWAYS BEEN A GREAT PROVIDER, SENPAI. YOU WERE BORN TO STAND ON THE SHOULDERS OF OTHER MEN!
HERE'S THE PLAN: BUTTER HIM UP, GET HIM DRUNK, AND MAKE HIM PAY THE BILL!
がはっがはっ
GA-HA-GA-HA!

I'VE FINALLY STARTED GETTING MORE GIRLS ON THE TEAM.
I'M THINKING IT'S ABOUT TIME WE SCHEDULED A MATCH.

YOU GOT A KENDO TEAM OVER THERE, RIGHT? LET'S GET SOMETHING SET UP!
A PRACTICE MATCH? SURE THING.
BUT I'VE ONLY GOT ONE MEMBER NOW, SO YOU'LL HAVE TO WAIT FOR MORE TO JOIN.

WANNA MAKE A BET...
...KOJIRO?

A BET?

RAAAAAAA!

SIGN: KENDO CLUB

HIYAH, HIYAH, HIYAH!
SUPAN
HIYAH, HOYAH, HOO-YAH!
SUPAN (THWACK)
WOW, THE KENDO TEAM'S CRAZY.
PAN (WHACK)
I'M SCARED!

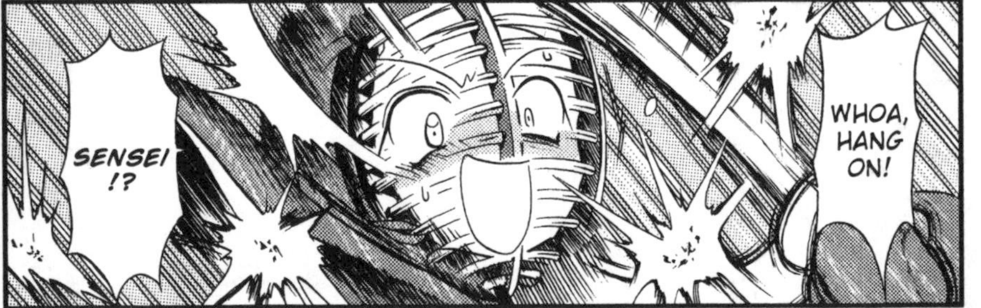

WHOA, HANG ON!
SENSEI !?

RAAAAHH!!

ARMOR: ISHIDA

ARMOR: CHIBA

I'M NOT GOING OVERBOARD! I'M JUST GETTING SERIOUS!
HAA (HUFF)
HAA
REMEMBER WHAT YOU SAID? WE'RE SHOOTIN' FOR THE STARS! THE NATIONAL CHAMPIONSHIP!
JIIN (TWINKLE)
SEN-SEI...
I'M PUT-TING MY ALL INTO PUMPING UP THIS CLUB!
AND WE AREN'T GONNA GET ANY NEW MEMBERS UNLESS OUR CAPTAIN'S AN ACE! THAT'S YOU!
OKAY! YOU CAN COUNT ON ME!
KIRA (SPARKLE)
KIRA
KIRA
WOW. IT'S LIKE LOOKING INTO A DIF-FERENT WORLD.
IT FEELS AWK-WARD TO GO IN.
EXCUSE US, WE'RE INTERESTED IN THE CLUB.
WE'D LIKE TO APPLY TO JOIN.
WE DON'T NEED BOYS, DAMMIT!!
EEEEK!

WHY WOULD YOU CHASE THEM AWAY LIKE THAT?
FU-FU-FU...
WE'RE FACING A GIRLS' TEAM! WHY WOULD I WANT MALE MEMBERS!?

"FAC-ING"?
AH.

OKAY, I'LL SPILL THE BEANS. WE'RE GONNA HAVE A LITTLE KENDO MEET AGAINST MY SENPAI'S STUDENTS!
I SEE.
BUT THEY'RE A GIRLS' TEAM, SO... WE CAN JUST TAKE IN SOME BOYS AFTER THAT!

I JUST NEED FIVE GIRLS FOR THE TEAM, THAT'S ALL!
WE CAN'T HAVE A MEET UNLESS WE FIELD A SQUAD!

A BET?

LOOK OUT, MY GIRLS ARE TOUGH!
BUT I'LL TELL YOU WHAT- IF YOU WIN...

...I'LL GIVE YOU A FULL YEAR OF MEALS AT MY DAD'S RESTAURANT... ON THE HOUSE.

ONE YEAR'S SUPPLY OF ALL-YOU-CAN-EAT, FREE, DELUXE, AUTHENTIC, TOKYO-STYLE SUSHI.
WEL-COME! COME ON IN!

HEH-HEH-HEH...I'LL USE EVERY DIRTY TRICK IN THE BOOK TO WIN...
THAT'S ONE YEAR...AND AN ENTIRE YEAR'S WORTH OF FOOD MONEY...HEH-HEH-HEH...

I'LL DO IT!! I'LL DO WHAT-EVER IT TAKES!!
THIS IS MY POCKET-BOOK ON THE LINE!!

SO... KIRINO, DO YOU HAVE ANY IDEAS? KNOW ANY KIDS FROM MIDDLE SCHOOL WHO DID KENDO?
'COS, UM, WE COULD REALLY USE THEM RIGHT ABOUT NOW.
HMM, YEAH, MAYBE JUST A FEW...

OH! HOW ABOUT THIS IDEA?
YOU GOT ONE? LAY IT ON ME!!

SFX: SHAKA (TIKA) KA KA KA

WE'LL LOOK AROUND FOR SOMEONE CARRYING WHAT LOOKS SORT OF LIKE A SHINAI...

THEN WE'LL THROW ROCKS AN' STUFF AT 'EM!
DOGYU (WHUSH)
DOGYU

AND IF THEY'RE REALLY GOOD WITH THE BLADE, THEY'LL KNOCK ALL THE ROCKS OUTTA THE AIR!!
WE'RE NOT IN A SAMURAI MOVIE.

ZA
ZA (SCRAPE)
WELL, WE'LL START WITH PEOPLE FROM YOUR MIDDLE SCHOOL.
SURE! I'LL ASK AROUND FOR THE FORMER KENDO TEAM MEM-BERS.
MAN, I CAN'T TELL YOU HOW GREAT IT IS THAT YOU'RE DOING ALL THIS FOR ME, SENSEI!
MWA-HA-HA!
BESHI (FWAP)
BASHI
HMM. MY HEART HURTS...
GUSA (STAB)
GUSA
LOOK OUT!
BASEBALL ON THE LOOSE!!
HYURURURU (SWIZZZ)
AND A TENNIS BALL FROM THE OTHER WAY!
RUGBY BALL!
THE VICE PRINCIPAL SLIPPED AND FELL FROM THE THIRD FLOOR!!

GA
GA
(WHACK)
GA

HYURURURU (SWEEEE)
ひゅるるる
ZAA (SPINN)
DO (WHOCK)
GASSHAAN (CRAAASH)

MY HEART WAS RACING.
IT RACED LIKE THE TIME I FELL IN LOVE AT FIRST SIGHT WITH THE GIRL FROM THE NEXT CLASS OVER IN MIDDLE SCHOOL...
I FORGOT ABOUT THE SUSHI. ALL I COULD THINK ABOUT WAS WHAT I'D JUST SEEN.
VICE PRINCI-PAL?
MR. VICE PRINCI-PAAAAL!!!

SIGN: ENI SUSHI

I'M NOT INTERESTED.
CHAPTER 2
NEW MEMBERS AND THE PING-PONG CLUB

I'M NOT INTERESTED.

LABEL: DOG GUIDEBOOK

SFX: KAN (CLANG) KAN

CHA (CHK)

BRRR! COLD ONE TONIGHT.

ALL THAT VENTING MADE ME HUNGRY.
TIME FOR SOME RAMEN.

BABABABA (BRRRMM)

HEADIN' OUT, KOJIRO? PERFECT TIMING.
BABABABA
YO, NOBU-CHAN. WANNA GET SOME RAMEN?

NAH, I'M ONLY HERE TO RETURN YOUR VIDEO.
AW, SHUCKS. YOU COULD DO THAT ANYTIME.

ACTUALLY, I WANTED TO CATCH YOU TO GET SOMETHING OF MINE BACK.
...WHAT, DID I BORROW SOMETHING?

MONEY.

M-MONEY?
YEP. MOOLA.
¥1,000... I HOPE?
NOPE, IT WAS 10,000.
...HERE YOU ARE...
GU
GU
GU (TUG)
LATER, MAN!
BABABA
LABEL: CUP RAMEN: SALT FLAVOR

LETTERS:
BILL / BILL / KOJIRO ISHIDA /
NOTICE OF DEFAULT

OKAY, THAT'S ALL FOR TODAY.
UHHH, AND YOU CAN TURN IN ALL THOSE WORKSHEETS NEXT TIME.

BOOOO (DUHH)

WAI (CHATTER)

YOU SEEM OUT OF IT TODAY, SEN-SEI.

LAY OFF! I'M STARVING.

WANT THIS BREAD, THEN? I COULDN'T FINISH IT AT LUNCH.
SWEET! I CAN HAVE IT!?
TAKE MINE TOO.

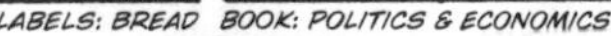
LABELS: BREAD BOOK: POLITICS & ECONOMICS

OH, HEY. HAS ANYONE HERE NOT DECIDED ON A CLUB YET?

SFX: HOKU (HUFF) HOKU

YOU'RE THE SUPER-VISOR OF THE KENDO CLUB?
YES, AND WE'RE LOOKING FOR MORE GIRLS TO JOIN.

IT SEEMS LIKE HE WOULD RUN A PRETTY LOW-KEY CLUB.
MAYBE WE SHOULD CHECK IT OUT.

RAAAHHH!!

SIGN: KENDO CLUB

SEIYA!
SEIYA!
SEIYA!

EEEEEEK!

GET UP! HOW CAN YOU EXPECT TO BE ON THE TEAM WITH THAT LACK OF DISCIPLINE!?
BUT... WE'VE NEVER DONE THIS BEFORE...

ARMOR: ISHIDA

I DON'T WANNA HEAR IT!!
YOU'RE NOT GONNA GET ANY TOUGHER WITH THAT KIND OF ATTITUDE! LIFE IS HARD, BRATS!!

SFX: HIIIIIIIII (EEEEEK)

IF YOU DON'T SEEK PERSONAL IMPROVEMENT, GET OUTTA MY FACE! RRRRAAGH!

ARMOR: ISHIDA

DAMN... THERE GO OUR HOPEFUL RECRUITS!
THE CLUB'S CONTINUED EXISTENCE IS IMPERILED!
I THINK WE'D DO BETTER IF YOU QUIT.

URO (LOITER) URO
OKAY, I DON'T CARE ABOUT THE GUYS, BUT I REALLY NEED SAYA...

SAYA!?

SILENCE! WHAT ABOUT THOSE OTHER MEMBERS, KIRINO!?
WHERE'S SAYA? WHERE ARE THE BOYS!?
I DUNNO, WHAT CAN I SAY...?
BESIDES, LOOK WHAT YOU DID ALREADY...

HELLO...
WE'D LIKE TO OBSERVE THE CLUB. IS THAT OKAY?
中田
GREAT, MORE GUYS...
SORRY, WE DON'T NEED ANY BOYS TODAY.
ドス
DOSU (THWAP)
LABEL (R): NAKATA
YOU'RE FIRST-YEARS, RIGHT? SURE, FEEL FREE TO WATCH!
I MEAN, HELL, JUST JOIN, Y'KNOW?
あっはっはっ
AH-HA-HA!
WRITE YOUR CLASS AND NAME RIGHT HERE.
OKAY.
NO FAIR, NAKATA-KUN!
YOU SAID WE'D JUST WATCH!
YOU PROMISED YOU'D GO AND CHECK OUT THE PING-PONG CLUB WITH ME LATER.
ぐいぐい
GUI GUI (TUG)
I KNOW, I KNOW! DON'T WORRY, I'LL GO WITH YOU, EIGA-KUN.

SFX: IRA (GRR) IRA IRA IRA

IF YOU DON'T WANT TO BE HERE, THEN YOU CAN JUST...
ドス
DOSU (BAM)
...TAKE IT EASY AND HAVE A GOOD TIME.

YOU'D BETTER! YOU PROMISED!
I'M SCARED TO GO ON MY OWN!
JUST GIVE ME A LITTLE LONGER, OKAY?

HA-HA. WELL, WE HAD THREE THIRD-YEARS, BUT THEY DROPPED OUT TO FOCUS ON THEIR COLLEGE ENTRANCE EXAMS.
ALSO, THERE ARE THREE OTHER SECOND-YEARS, LIKE ME.

...WHERE ARE THE OTHER PEOPLE?
OR IS THIS IT?

SFX: IRA IRA IRA IRA IRA
SFX: KUOO (AAGH)

AWWWWWW...
WHY ARE THERE SO FEW PEOPLE HERE?

IT'S MORE FUN WITH LOTS AND LOTS OF PEOPLE!
C'MON, LET'S JOIN THE PING-PONG CLUB!
I DON'T KNOW ABOUT THAT...

...I REALLY LIKE KENDO.

I'LL COME BACK LATER SINCE IT SEEMS PRETTY EMPTY FOR TODAY.
HURRY, NAKATA-KUN!

SAY, KIRINO...
WUZZUP, SENSEI?

I MAKE A TERRIBLE TEACHER ...
I'VE ONLY BEEN THINKING ABOUT MYSELF...
TOOK YOU LONG ENOUGH, HUH?

BUT... YOU KNOW HOW IT GOES, RIGHT?
LIFE MAKES YOU HUNGRY ...YOU KNOW?

AND SUSHI... SUSHI'S GOT THIS MAGICAL POWER.
YOU KNOW? A MAGICAL POWER OF TEMPTATION.
A MYSTERICAL, MAGICAMAL POWER.
......
PARDON?

ALL RIGHT, TAMAKI-CHAN! TODAY'S THE DAY YOU...

BEGIN!

SUPA
(SWACK)

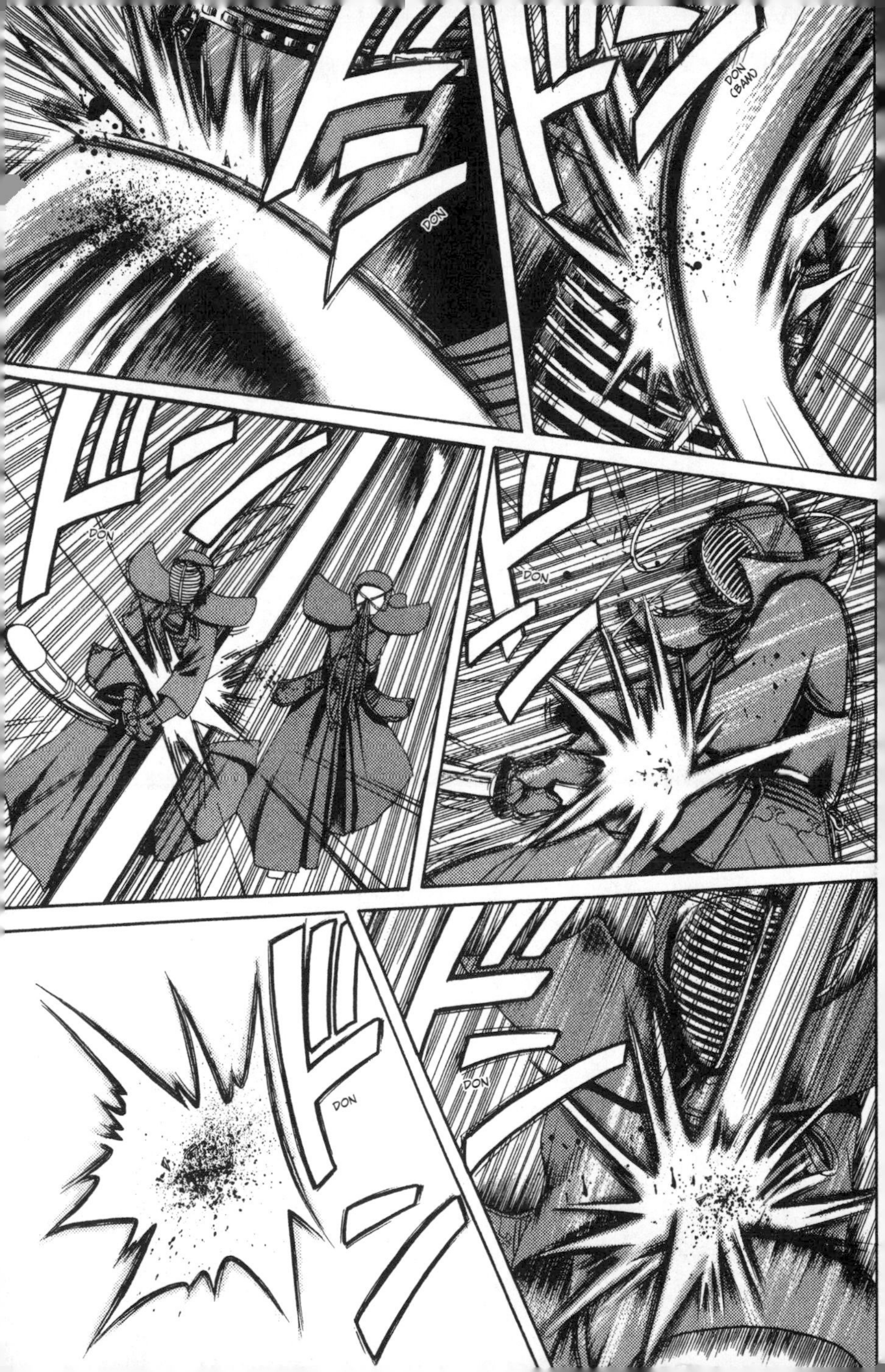
DON
(BAM)
DON
DON
DON
DON
DON

HAA
HAA (HUFF)
HÂA
HA'A
HÂA
HAA
HAA
ARMOR: ANDO

THAT'S GOOD. ENOUGH FOR TODAY, TAMAKI.
YOU CAN WRAP UP AND SEE TO YOUR STUDIES.

THANK YOU FOR THE LESSON.

AND AGAIN, **NOT A DROP OF SWEAT...**

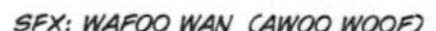

SFX: BABABAU BABABAU (WOWOWOOF WOWOWOOF)

....
MOGU
(MUNCH)
MOGU
もぐもぐ

...JOINING THE KENDO CLUB AT SCHOOL?
コト
KOTO (TNK)

......?
WHY WOULD I DO THAT?

...WELL, BECAUSE...
I DO IT EVERY DAY AT HOME.

YES, BUT...
...I THINK YOU MIGHT HAVE FUN... DOING IT AT SCHOOL.

FUN ...?

......?

WELL ...
THAT'S OKAY.

SFX: KACHA

ジャー
JAAAA (CREAK)
カチャ
KACHA
カチャ
KACHA

I'M GOING TO MY ROOM NOW.
I'LL WASH THE DISHES LATER... JUST SOAK THEM IN THE SINK.
ALL RIGHT.

......
......
スタ SUTA (TMP)
スタ SUTA

WELL, HONEY ...
...IT'S HARD RAISING A TEENAGE DAUGHTER.
I'M SURE IT'S HARD WITH EVERY GIRL...
...BUT OURS ESPE-CIALLY...

WELL, I KNOW ONE THING...
...WE COULD USE A SMALLER TABLE.

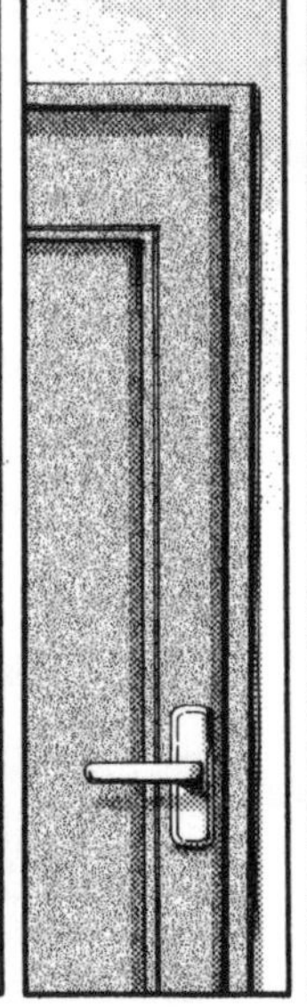

OH...

SIGN: COMEDY HOUR

ひょい
HYOI (ZWIP)
HI, I'M NAKATA! I VISITED YESTER-DAY...

EXCELLENT! SO GOOD OF YOU TO RETURN!!
WRITE YOUR CLASS AND NAME!!
DO
DO
DO (STOMP)
DO
BIKU (FLINCH)

HUH...?
IS THAT THE SAME GUY?

YEAH, HE'S TAGGING ALONG AGAIN.
WELL, THAT'S FINE, BUT...

SFX: U (SOB) U

...WHY IS HE CRYING ...?

IT TURNS OUT...

...THERE IS NO PING-PONG CLUB...

HEY... DON'T LET LIFE GET YOU DOWN!
YOU SHOULD JOIN THE KENDO CLUB TOO!

ARMOR: CHIBA
ARMOR: ISHIDA

BUT I'VE NEVER DONE KENDO BEFORE ...
NO SWEAT! IT'S LIKE YOUR PADDLE TURNS INTO A SHINAI! THEY'RE BOTH MADE OF WOOD, RIGHT?
NOW THAT'S JUST CRUEL, KIRINO...

NO, IT'S OKAY... I'D RATHER MAKE A PING-PONG CLUB ALL BY MYSELF...
C'MON, GIVE IT A SHOT.
FURA (WOBBLE)

YOU DON'T KNOW HOW YOU'LL FEEL ABOUT IT UNTIL YOU TRY.
KENDO'S PRETTY FUN.
NI (GRIN)

ANYWAY... NAKATA-KUN, RIGHT?
GOT A GIRL-FRIEND?
WHY DON'CHA ASK HER TO JOIN THE KENDO CLUB WITH YA?
GASHI (SQUEEZE)
ARMOR: ISHIDA

SORRY, I DON'T HAVE ONE!
I'LL ASK THE GIRLS IN MY CLASS, THOUGH.

I CAN INVITE MY GIRLFRIEND TO JOIN.
SHE PROBABLY HASN'T JOINED A CLUB YET.

YOU'VE GOT A GIRL-FRIEND!?

Illustration:Aguri Igarashi

Illustration:Masahiro Totsuka

MUROE PRIVATE SENIOR HIGH SCHOOL.

SIGN: KENDO CLUB

SIGN: ULTRA-SEEKING NEW MEMBERS!! GET IN HERE!

MUS-CLE TRAIN-ING?
WHY WOULD WE DO THAT? THAT SUCKS!

I WANNA HOLD A SHINAI!
LEMME SWING A SHINAI!

NEW MEMBERS DO MUSCLE TRAINING UNTIL SUMMER! AND YOU DON'T GET TO USE A SHINAI UNTIL AFTER TRAINING!
ZUBISHI (ZWAP)
DENIED !!!
AWW!

FURTHER-MORE, WHEN PRACTICE IS OVER, FIRST-YEARS HAVE TO WIPE DOWN THE FLOOR!!
PISHI (WHAP) PASHI
BUT WE ONLY HAVE TWO FIRST-YEARS...
FLOOR! "YUKA"! CAPISCE?

GOOD POINT, WHICH IS WHY I'LL BE HELPING YOU TWO UNTIL WE GET A HEALTHIER STOCK OF NEW KIDS!
DON'T SWEAT IT. I MEAN, LOOK AT OUR SUPER-VISOR.
THIS DUDE.

SIGN: VICTORY

ARMOR: CHIBA

WHEN ARE THE OTHER SENPAI GOING TO COME?
HA-HA! WHO KNOWS?

PLUS, KOJIRO-SENSEI SAID HE HAD TO LOOK INTO SOME-THING TODAY.
IT'S JUST US, SO LET'S TAKE IT EASY!
WAI (WHEE) WAI
OKAY.

OH, I GUESS I SHOULD INTRODUCE MYSELF.

I'M KIRINO, THE TEAM CAPTAIN.
KIRINO CHIBA. NICE TO MEET YOU!
CHAPTER 3
KOJIRO & THE MOST VALUABLE THING

SHA (SHHK)
SU (SFF)
GYU (SWOP)
I'LL HAVE TO ORDER A STANDARD HIGH SCHOOL SHINAI SOON.
BUN (WHOOSH)
NO FAIR! HOW COME YUJI GETS TO HOLD A SHINAI AND SWING A SHINAI!?
PUNSUKA (HARRUMPH)
NAKATA-KUN'S OKAY 'COS HE'S DONE THIS BEFORE!
YOU LOOK LIKE YOU'RE BETTER THAN ME!
HOW LONG HAVE YOU DONE IT?
I WAS IN THE KENDO CLUB ALL THREE YEARS OF MIDDLE SCHOOL.
ALSO, I WENT TO A KENDO DOJO IN GRADE SCHOOL.
REALLY? WHAT DOJO?

KAWAZOE DOJO.

WHAT DID YOU JUST SAY!!!?

BAKON (THWAM)

KOJIRO-SENSEI!

YOUR VOLUME'S MORE OUT OF CONTROL THAN EVER.

KAWAZOE DOJO...!?

TANA-
KA-
KUN!
UH, IT'S
NAKATA.

YOU'RE ON
THE TEAM!
I KNEW I
WAS RIGHT
TO RECRUIT
YOU!
ACTUALLY,
I VOLUN-
TEERED
TO JOIN...

SENSEI,
I WANNA
PUT
GUARDS
ON AND
SWING A
SHINAI!
NYOOOO
(BLERRR)
HUH? OH,
WHATEVER!
HAVE FUN!
KNOCK
YOURSELF
OUT!

NIKO
(GRIN)
GASHI
(GRAB)

I'M
GONNA
BORROW
NAKATA-
KUN FOR
A BIT,
KIRINO!!!
DAAAA
(ZOOOOM)
EEEEEEK!!

.....
I NEED
GUARDS,
SENPAI!

WHEN'S THE LAST TIME YOU VISITED?
I HAVEN'T BEEN TO THE DOJO SINCE I STARTED MIDDLE SCHOOL.
BUT WHAT'S THE BIG DEAL?

THERE WAS A GIRL ABOUT YOUR AGE THERE, RIGHT?
OH, YOU MEAN TAMA-CHAN?

TAMA-CHAN! YES!!
TAMAKI KAWAZOE, CLASS 1-9!!

AS A MATTER OF FACT, I WAS LATE TODAY BECAUSE I WAS DIGGING UP DIRT ON HER!
DIGGING UP DIRT...? YIKES! THIS TEACHER SEEMS SORT OF UNBAL-ANCED...

THE DAUGHTER OF THE DOJO! NO WONDER!
I NEED HER FOR THE TEAM. I GOTTA HAVE HER!

HELP ME, NAKATA! GET TAMAKI KAWAZOE ON THE KENDO TEAM ANY WAY YOU CAN!
GAKU (SHAKE) GAKU
YOU WANT TAMA-CHAN? I DON'T THINK SHE'LL COME.
SHE DOESN'T LIKE THIS STUFF.

WE WENT TO THE SAME MIDDLE SCHOOL, SO I ASKED HER TO JOIN THE KENDO CLUB THERE.
AND ALL SHE SAID WAS, "WHY?"

TO HER, KENDO IS LIKE A HOUSEHOLD CHORE SHE HAS TO COMPLETE ...
SHE DOESN'T DO IT BECAUSE SHE LIKES IT.

......

WHEN WE PICKED P.E. SUBJECTS, SHE NEVER CHOSE KENDO.
IN FACT, I'VE NEVER HEARD HER MENTION THE WORD "KENDO" AT SCHOOL.

BUT SHE DOESN'T HATE IT... RIGHT?
NO... I JUST DON'T THINK IT'S LIKELY SHE'LL JOIN.

...
...SO THAT'S WHAT WE'RE DEALING WITH...

SO, HOW TO GET HER TO JOIN...
WOW... YOU'RE REALLY SERIOUS ABOUT THIS...

I CAN'T GET THINGS START-ED WITH-OUT HER...
IN FACT, IF I DON'T HAVE HER, EV-ERYTHING IS LOST...

WHAT ...?
SERIOUS!
DANGER!
DIS-BANDING!
WHAT'S THE PROBLEM? CAN YOU TELL ME?

THIS STIIIIIIII-IIIIIIINKS!

THESE GUARDS ALL STINK! I CAN'T WEAR THEM!
THEY PROBABLY HAVE MOLD GROWING ON THEM!
*MOAAAA (WHUFFF)
HA-HA-HA! YOU BET THEY DO!

THEY'RE PRETTY OLD, YOU KNOW! YOU'LL HAVE TO WAIT FOR US TO ORDER NEW ONES.
WHAAAAAAT?

ARMOR: CHIBA

COMMON FACTS OF KENDO

• ITEMS LYING AROUND THE ROOM WILL BE SMELLY; BE CAREFUL.

• JABBING PEOPLE NOT WEARING GUARDS IS DANGEROUS AND CAN CAUSE DEATH; BE CAREFUL.

SUSHI...?
YEAH! JUST BEAT MY SENPAI'S STUDENTS, AND I'LL GET A WHOLE YEAR'S WORTH, FREE!
ISN'T THAT AWESOME!? COULD IT GET ANY BETTER!?
THAT'S A BOLD WAGER! HE MUST HAVE TOTAL CONFIDENCE THAT HE'S GONNA WIN!
HIS TEAM MUST BE DAMN GOOD!
THAT'S WHY I NEED TAMAKI KAWAZOE! SHE'S WORTH A WHOLE YEAR OF THE SUSHI LIFE!
MY LIFE-STYLE—NAY, MY VERY LIFE—DEPENDS ON HER!
WOW... WOW...
HE SURE THINKS HE CAN BEAT ME, THAT RAT...
BOY, I CAN'T WAIT TO SEE HIS FACE WHEN WE CLOBBER HIM...
WHAT A TERRIBLE MAN...
WHAT A HORRIBLE, WORTHLESS ADULT...

HE'S LIKE THE MODEL FOR EVERYTHING WRONG WITH ADULTHOOD. I'LL NEVER BE LIKE HIM.
WHAT A SCUMBAG. WHAT A BAD, BAD, VERY BAD MAN...
ONLY CONCERNED WITH HIS OWN MATTERS, NOT WITH HIS STUDENTS...
BLAH BLAH BLAH MONEY.
BLAH BLAH BLAH FOOD.
SO YOU SEE, NAKATA! MY WALLET DEPENDS ON YOU!
I MUST HAVE TAMAKI KAWA-ZOE!
I...I CAN'T!
HELL, I'LL LET YOU HAVE SOME SUSHI TOO!
JUST DON'T TELL ANYONE ELSE ABOUT THIS!
R-RIGHT...
OKAY, RAMEN'S ON ME!
LET'S GO HAMMER OUT A PLAN!
C-CAN I JUST GO HOME IN-STEAD?
PURURURURU (RING)
SPEAK OF THE DEVIL.
IT'S SENPAI!
PI (BEEP)

YO, KOJIRO.

YOU GOT SOME TIME?

YEAH, I REMEMBER THE BET.

HA-HA, I WASN'T THAT DRUNK!

SIGN: KENDO CLUB

IF MY SCHOOL WINS...
...I'M GONNA TAKE THAT THING YOU'VE GOT IN YOUR ROOM.
HUH? WHAT'S IN MY ROOM...?
You know... the most valuable thing you've got.
MOST VALUABLE THING...
モヤモヤ
MOYA MOYA (FWOOOO)
MY SNES!?
NO !!
The trophy!
TRO ...
...FEEEEEE?

EXACTLY... THAT BELONGED TO ME ORIGINALLY.
IF I WIN, I WANT IT BACK.
THERE'S NO USE YOU AND ME FIGHTING FOR IT, SO WE'LL LET OUR PUPILS DO THE WORK...
Got that, Kojiro?
The prizes are sushi for you, the trophy for me!
PUTSU (CLICK)
PUUUU (BOOOP)
PUUUU
PUUUU

NOW... I REALLY HAVE TO WIN THIS MEET.

タナカ薬局
SIGN: ENGLISH LESSONS
SIGN: TANAKA PHARMACY
シャー
SHAAAA (FZZZZZ)
LABEL: BIKE LANE
TAMA-CHAN!
CHIRIRIN (RING RING)

LABELS: EVIL SLAYER

OH, YUJI-KUN.

I WISH YOU'D STOP CALLING ME TAMA-CHAN.
I'M IN HIGH SCHOOL NOW.

CHIRIRIN (RING RING)

HMM.

IT IS KIND OF A SHAME, THOUGH.

SURE, SHE MIGHT BE A NORMAL TEENAGE GIRL (A LITTLE ON THE SMALL SIDE)...
...BUT WHEN SHE HOLDS A SHINAI...

...SHE'S INVINCIBLE.
CHAPTER 4
TOYAMA & IWASA

KI (SKREE)

HUH? WELL, IF I DON'T CALL HER TAMA-CHAN...
WHAT SHOULD I CALL HER?

KAWA-ZOE?
TAMA-KI...?
TAMA...
TAMA...

BLAH, FOR-GET IT.
TAMA-CHAN WORKS FINE ENOUGH.
CHIRIRIN (RING RING)

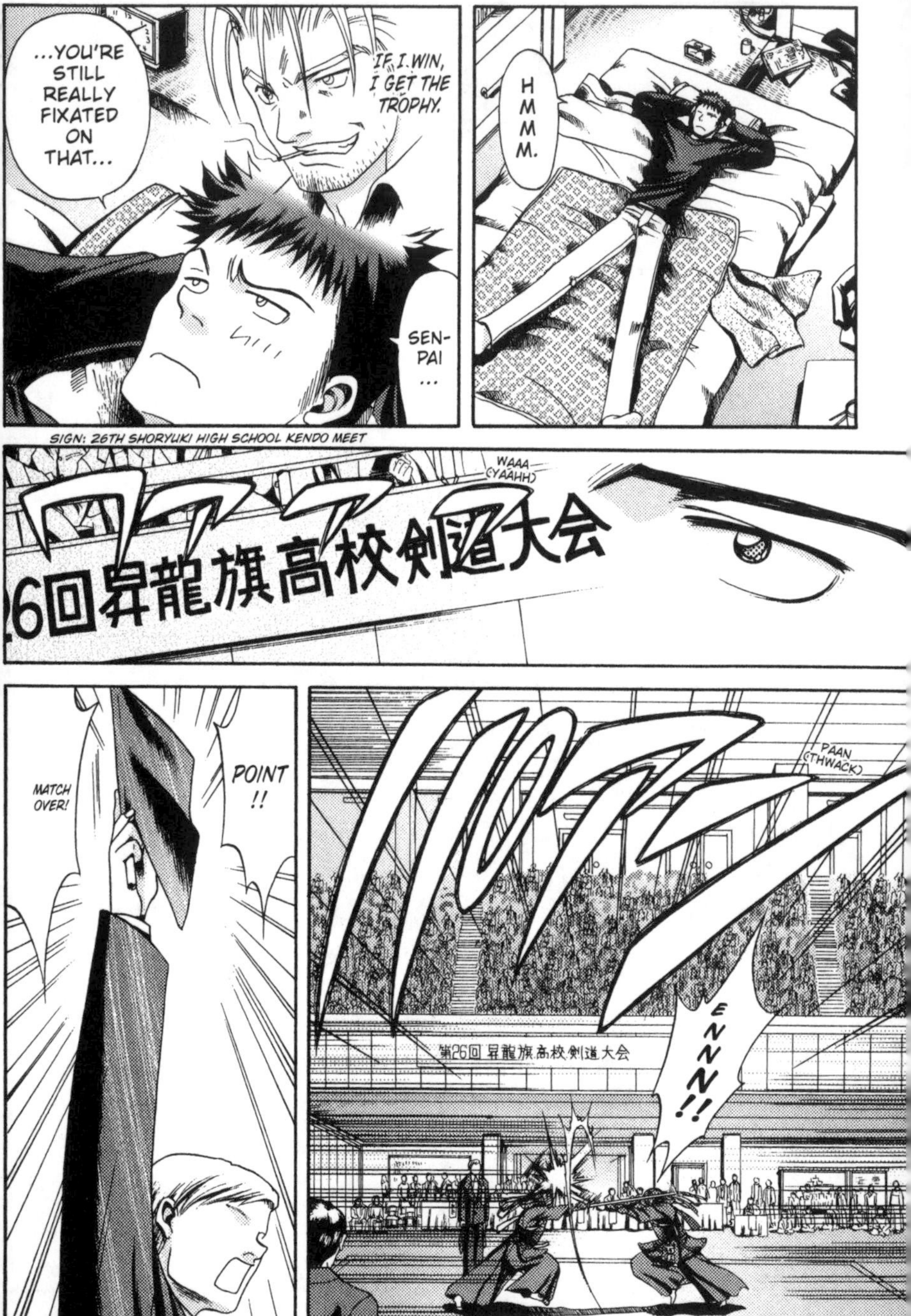

IF I WIN, I GET THE TROPHY.
...YOU'RE STILL REALLY FIXATED ON THAT...
SEN-PAI...

SIGN: 26TH SHORYUKI HIGH SCHOOL KENDO MEET

PAAN (THWACK)

ENNN!!

第26回昇龍旗高校剣道大会

POINT !!

MATCH OVER!

HE DID IT!
KOJIRO WON IT ALL!
YEAAAAAH!
HAA (HUFF)
HAA

HAA
HAA

I'M SORRY, SENPAI! THAT ONE GOT IN THERE BY SHEER LUCK.
IT WAS ALL LUCK; THAT WAS THE ONLY REASON I WON.
KOJIRO...

... YOU'RE WRONG ...

LUCK OR SKILL, THE RESULT IS EVERY-THING.
YOU WON, FAIR AND SQUARE.

THANKS!!
AND THAT WAS THE LAST TIME SENPAI AND I DUELED...
BUT THEN...

SAY, KOJIRO.

I-I-I-I-I-I-I-I-

I DON'T CARE ABOUT THAT AT AAAA-AALL!!

UHH...

DAAAA (ZOOOM)

UH-OH...

AND EVER SINCE THEN...

HEY, KOJIRO, HOW'S THE TROPHY HOLDING UP?

WANNA PUT THAT TROPHY IN THE POT?

HA! JUST KID-DING.

YOUR EYES AREN'T ...

BUT THAT WASN'T A MATCH BETWEEN BEGINNERS...

YOU DON'T WIN WITH LUCK IN KENDO. A WEAK MAN DOESN'T BEAT A STRONG MAN BY CHANCE.

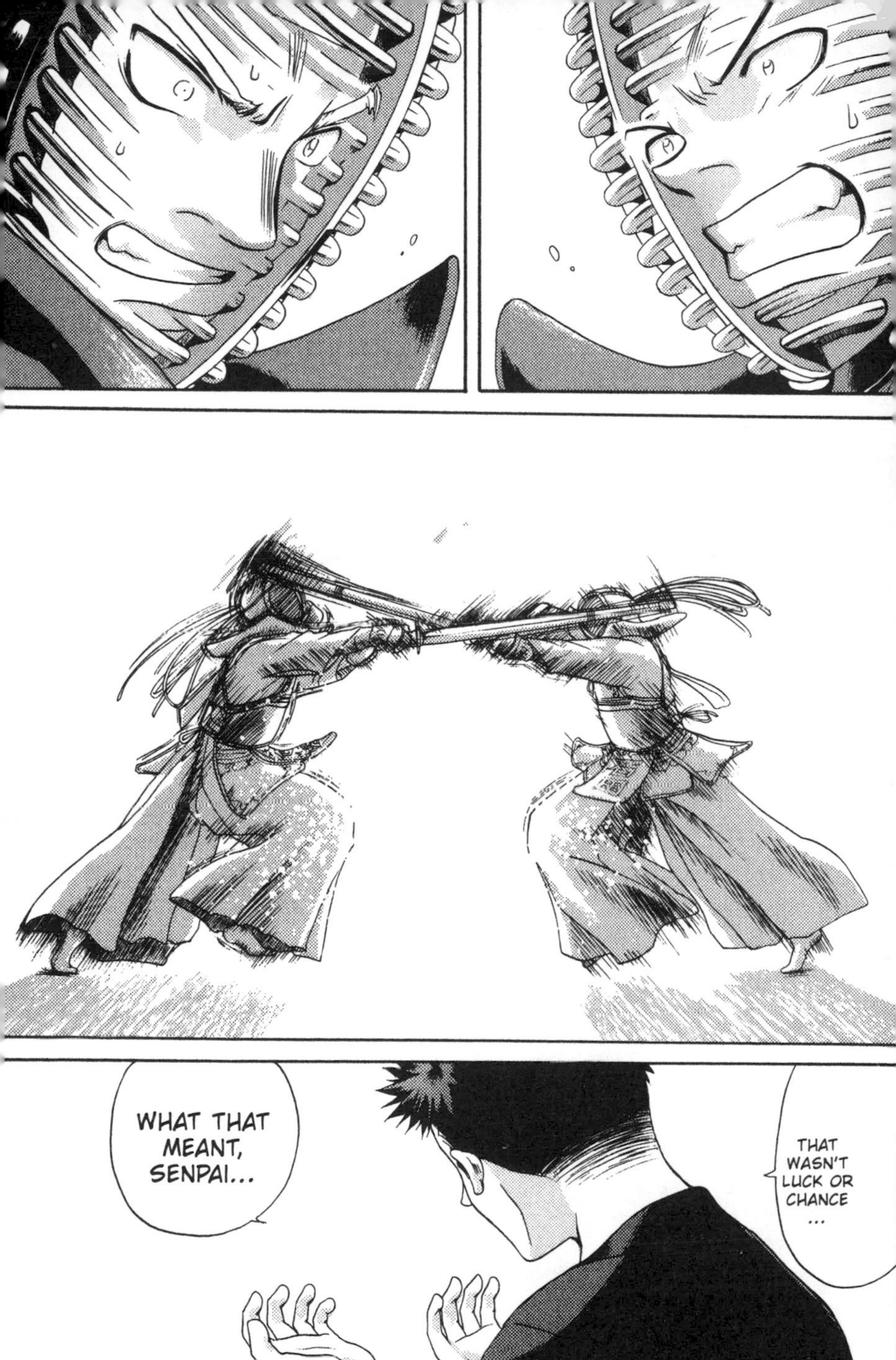
THAT WASN'T LUCK OR CHANCE ...
WHAT THAT MEANT, SENPAI...

...WAS THAT I WAS STRONGER THAN YOU...

KOFF!

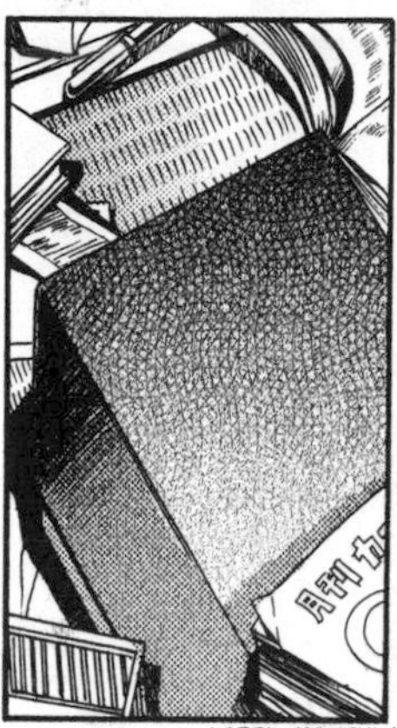

LABEL: MONTHLY

HERE'S THAT TROPHY!

IT'S NOT LIKE I KEEP IT DISPLAYED ON MY SHELF, SENPAI.

IN FACT, IT'S ONLY HERE BECAUSE IT GOT LUMPED IN WITH A BUNCH OF OTHER JUNK WHEN I MOVED OUT...

THIS THING DOESN'T MEAN ANY-THING TO ME...
...BUT...

I STILL CAN'T AFFORD TO LOSE...

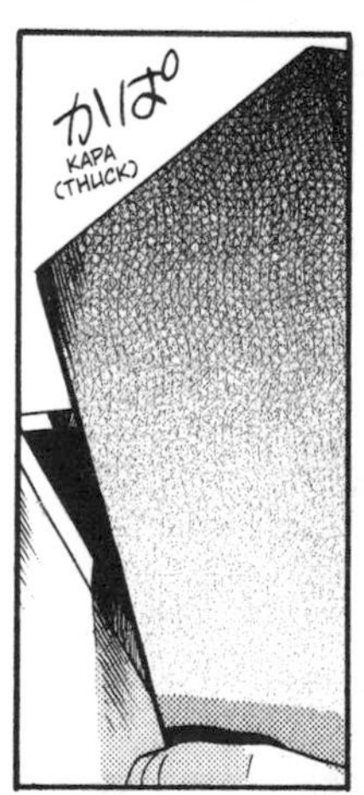
かぱ
KAPA (THUCK)

TROPHY: 26TH SHORYUKI HIGH SCHOOL KENDO MEET INDIVIDUAL CHAMPION

...BECAUSE I TOTALLY SMASHED THE TROPHY TO PIECES!!
GAN (WHACK)
HIYAH! HIYAH!
GAN
BEKI (CRNK)
KASA (TIKA) KASA
ALL BECAUSE I SAW A COCKROACH AND TRIED TO KILL IT...

HE'S GONNA BE REALLY PISSED IF HE FINDS OUT...

THIS IS WHY I CAN'T AFFORD TO LOSE THIS BET!
わんわん わん
WAN (WOOF) WAN WAN

LABEL: MEMBERS!

......
KIRINO! YUJI!
BE HONEST. WHAT DO YOU THINK SHE'LL BE LIKE?
I'M THINKING...
空想
ILLUSION
夢
DREAM
幻影
IMAGINARY
バーチャル
VIRTUAL
SHE MIGHT NOT EVEN TECHNICALLY BE HUMAN... SHE COULD BE SOME SORT OF IMAGINARY CONCEPTUAL GIRLFRIEND THAT EXISTS ONLY INSIDE HIS HEAD...
ERRR, I'M INCLINED TO THINK SHE'S JUST A NORMAL GIRL.
BUT PROBABLY CLOSER TO A "GIRL-FRIEND" THAN A "GIRLFRIEND."
NORMAL
NO WAY. I KNOW GUYS LIKE THAT...
ちっちっちっ
CHI (TSK) CHI CHI
THEY ALWAYS PULL IN THE REAL SPARKLY-GLITTERY TYPE.
キラキラー
SPARKLY
キュピーン
GLITTERY

PRETTY BOY/ PRETTY GIRL COUPLES TOTALLY SUCK!
THEY IRRITATE ME AND MAKE ME SAD!
HERE'S WHAT I THINK...

I SEE! YOU'VE GOT A POINT, KIRINO!
I'M SURE OF IT!
ARE YOU GUYS SERIOUS?

A COUPLE SHOULD TOTAL 100 POINTS, NO MORE!
THERE NEEDS TO BE A BALANCE BETWEEN THE TWO!!

A 30-POINT GUY WITH A 70-POINT GIRL!
A 10-POINT GIRL WITH A 90-POINT GUY!
IT WOULD REALLY HELP WITH BRIDGING THE WORLD'S GROWING ATTRACTIVENESS GAP, DON'T YOU THINK!?
HE'S WAY MORE INTO THIS THAN THE CLASS LESSONS...

......WHICH IS WHY I'M GUESSING...
...HE'LL PROBABLY BRING IN A GIRL LIKE THIS...
KIRA (SPARKLE) KIRA
I DON'T KNOW...

WE'RE HERE, YOU GUYS!
I BROUGHT MIYA-MIYA!
IT'S NICE TO MEET YOU. MY NAME IS MIYAKO MIYAZAKI.
YOU HAVE TO BE SHITTING ME!!!!

2-1

WHATCHA LOOKIN' FOR, TOYAMA?

LET'S GO, MAN.

IT'S GONE.

WHAT IS?

MY CELL.
BWA-HA-HA! HOW'D YOU LOSE THAT?

IT WAS PROBABLY MY LAST CLASS.
THAT'S THE COMMUNICATIONS ROOM. COME WITH, IWASA.
HELL NO. YOU LOST IT, YOU GET IT.

DAMN!

UMM... TOYAMA-KUN.

THIS IS YOUR CELL PHONE, RIGHT?

SORRY... I PICKED IT UP BY ACCIDENT LAST PERIOD.
IT'S THE SAME MODEL AS MINE...

HEY, TAKASUGI.

URRG...

DO (WHAM)

GOTTA GET THE CLUB SIGN-UP SHEETS!
たたた
TA (STPP) TA TA

THAT WAS MESSED UP, MAN.
UGH ...
HACK ...

HEY, IT'S KOJIRO.
IWASA! TOYAMA!

QUIT SLACKIN' OFF AND COME TO PRACTICE!
JUST SHOW UP IF YOU DON'T HAVE ANYTHING BETTER TO DO!

YEAH, YEAH.
WE'RE BUSY TODAY.
BUSY BEING LAZY, MORE LIKE IT.

WHAT-EVER.
I DON'T HAVE TIME TO MESS WITH THEM!

ON THE OTHER HAND, THE GIRLS WILL NEED PART-NERS TO PRACTICE WITH...
BUT WILL THOSE TWO TAKE IT SERI-OUSLY?

IT'S A GOOD THING KOJIRO'S OUR SUPER-VISOR.
HE'S SO CHILL.
YEAH.

ぴた…
PITA (STOP)

...
WAIT A SEC ...

I'VE GOT AN IDEA...
TO HER, KENDO IS LIKE A HOUSEHOLD CHORE SHE HAS TO COMPLETE...
IN FACT, I'VE NEVER HEARD HER MENTION THE WORD "KENDO" AT SCHOOL.
SFX: GA (WHACK) GA GA
SO WHY WAS SHE SWINGING THE BROOM AROUND LIKE THAT?
IWASA...
TOYAMA...

I CAN USE THEM!!

SFX: IRA (UGH) IRA IRA IRA IRA IRA IRA IRA IRA

LOOK, SEE? THIS IS HOW YOU HOLD A SHINAI!
OOH, DAN-KUN, YOU'RE SO COOL!

Illustration:Aguri Igarashi

Illustration:Masahiro Totsuka

...I GOT INTO A BIG FIGHT WITH SOME OLDER KIDS.

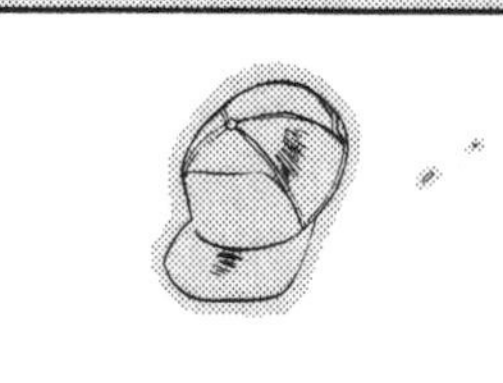

BUN
(WHACK)
AAAAH!

WHAT THE HECK DO YOU THINK YOU'RE DOING!? DON'T SWING THAT THING AROUND!!

IT'S NOT MY PROB-LEM!

カッ
KA
(TAKK)

!?

THAT'S WHEN SHE SHOWED UP.

MY HERO ...

TAMAKI KAWA-ZOE...

THAT'S RIGHT. TAMA-CHAN.

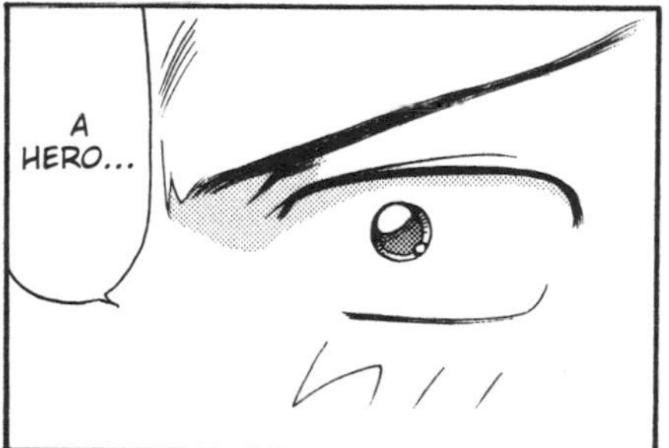
A HERO...

YOU STU-PID...
BA (SNAK)
BUN (WHIFF) -BUN

BISHI (WHACK)
YEOW!

STOP THAT, RIGHT NOW!!!
CHAPTER 5
TOYAMA AND HIS SHOES

...YOU LITTLE...
NO!!
BUN (CHUCK)
KAN (KLAK)

SHE'S NORMALLY VERY QUIET.
BUT AT TIMES LIKE THAT, SHE COMES FORWARD TO HELP.
SHE LIKES IT, IN FACT!

IT MUST BE SOMETHING SHE'S ALWAYS WANTED TO DO...
SHE ALWAYS DID LIKE STORIES WITH HEROES...

HEROES...

OH, AND BY THE WAY...
ガン
GAN (GONK)
...THIS IS THE SCAR FROM THE ROCK SHE DEFLECTED.

I'VE GOT A HANDLE ON HER NOW!!

I JUST HAVE TO MAKE USE OF HER CHARACTER!
KAKI (SCRIBBLE) KAKI
HEH-HEH-HEH! JUST WAIT 'TIL I BANG OUT THIS SCRIPT FOR GETTING TAMAKI KAWAZOE IN THE CLUB!!
I DID IT ALL FOR THE SUSHI!!
GOOOO (WHOOOMM)
ISHIDA-KUN? PIPE DOWN.

LABEL: 3-4 ATTENDANCE

FUUU (WHEWW)

PLEASE, MIYAKO.
CAN'T YOU WAIT UNTIL AFTER SCHOOL?
HMM?

WELL, I CAN'T SMOKE IN FRONT OF MY BOY-FRIEND, SO...
OH, TELL ME IF A TEACHER'S COMING.

SPEAKING OF YOUR BOYFRIEND, I HEARD YOU JOINED THE SAME CLUB AS HIM.
WHICH ONE?
たったった
TA (TMP) TA TA

MIYA-MIYA!
たったった
TA TA TA
WHERE ARE YOUUU?
!!

TAKE THIS!
MMF !?

OVER HERE, DAN-KUN!
ひょいっ
HYOI (ZOIP)
LET'S GO TO THE CLUB, MIYA-MIYA.

ゲホ
GEHO (COFF)
キャッ キャッ
KYA KYA (HEE-HEE)
COME ON, MIYA-MIYA!
DON (THUMP)
THAT HURT!
OH... I'M SORRY.

DOKA (CRACK)

WAIT UP.
ZA (SHFF)

OWWW... OH, THAT HURT ...!!
W-WHY DID YOU DO THAT?

HAH! YOU JUST GOT YOUR BRAND NEW SHOES STEPPED ON!
YOU DESERVE ANOTHER KICK.

SIGN: MARTIAL ARTS HALL

OYO?
THAT LOOKS LIKE...
...TAMA-CHAAAN!
OVER HERE! ♡
たたたっ TA (TMP) TA TA
...?
OH, RIGHT! I'M KIRINO CHIBA! I'M THE CAPTAIN OF THE KENDO TEAM.
NICE TO MEET YOU! HOW ABOUT YOU, HAVE YOU PICKED OUT A CLUB? THINKING ABOUT KENDO?
I DON'T THINK I...
OH, I KNOW! IT'S SO HARD TO CHOOSE!
BUT I'M NOT...
たたたっ
TATATA
YOU'LL JUST HAVE TO COME ALONG AND OB-SERVE THE CLUB TO SEE WHAT YOU THINK!
ふぉっほっほっ♪
BWA-HA-HA!

PAAN (THWACK)

DAN (WHAM)

YOU'RE HURT-ING ME...

ON YOUR FEET, EIGA-KUN.
YOUR SENPAI IS GIVING YOU A LESSON.

WHAT DO YOU WANT TO LEARN NEXT?
HOW TO STRIKE A GAUNT-LET?

THAT ASSHOLE...!!

STOP THIS PRAC-TICE! IT'S CRUEL!
THERE, THERE.

BASHI (FWAP)
EYACK!!

IS HE AIMING FOR THE CRACKS IN BETWEEN THE GUARDS!?
THERE, THERE.

TOYA-MA-KUN.

HEY, KIRINO. I HEAR YOU'RE THE CAPTAIN NOW.
COME ON NOW, TOYAMA-KUN. YOU CAN'T JUST COME BACK AND START HARASSING THE NEW KIDS.

WE'RE BOYS, YOU'RE GIRLS.
WE DO THINGS OUR WAY, YOU DO THINGS YOUR WAY.
GUI (TUG) グイ
GET UP, EIGA-KUN.

WE DON'T WANT TO INTER-RUPT THE GIRLS, DO WE? LET'S GO IN THE CORNER.
WE'LL PRAC-TICE OUR JABS NEXT.
TOYA-MA-KUN!

GREAT... MAYBE I SHOULD CALL FOR KOJIRO-SENSEI.
CAN I ASK SOME-THING?

WHY IS HE PUSHING YOU AROUND IF YOU'RE THE CAPTAIN?

TECHNI-CALLY, HE'S THE BEST IN THE CLUB.
BUT A LOT OF PEOPLE HAVE QUIT ON ACCOUNT OF HIM.
HE'S PUSHING EVERYONE AROUND... BECAUSE HE'S THE BEST?

...I SEE ...

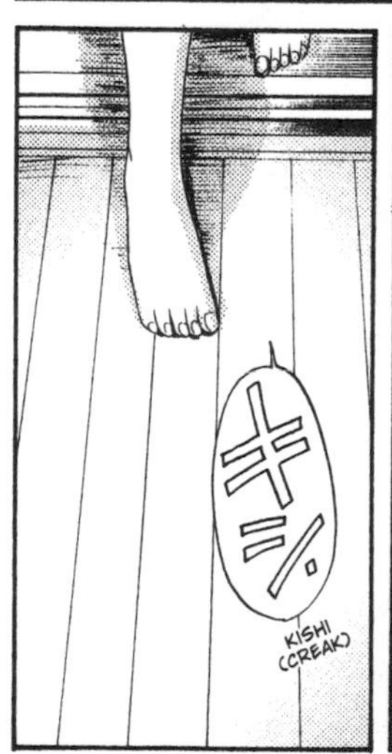
KISHI (CREAK)

I'D LIKE TO JOIN TEMPORARILY, JUST FOR A BIT.

...IT'S BAD GUYS!

SIGN: KENDO CLUB

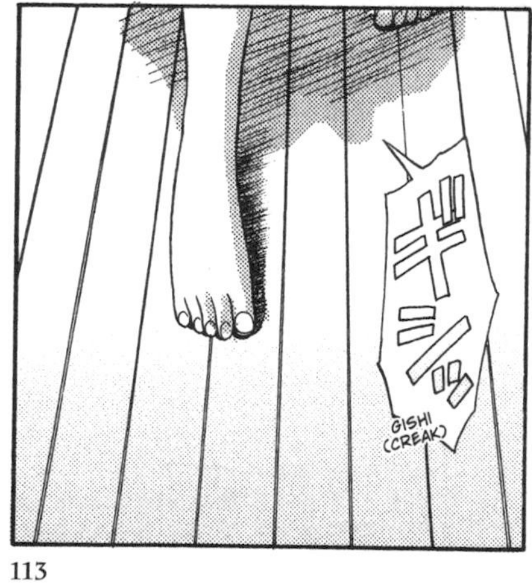

ギシッ
GISHI (CREAK)

WHO'S THIS?
A NEW MEM-BER?

THAT'S RIGHT, TOYAMA-KUN. BE NICE!
THIS IS TAMAKI KAWAZOE-CHAN. SHE'S IN HER FIRST YEAR HERE, BUT SHE'S DONE KENDO BEFORE.

I SEE.

GO ON, GET CHANGED.

YOU'VE DONE THIS BEFORE, RIGHT?

YOU CAN PUT GUARDS ON. IT'S COOL.

BUN (WHFF)

I'LL GIVE YOU A TEST.

CHAPTER 6
TOYAMA AND THE CARBON SHINAI
室江高
ARMOR: MUROE HIGH

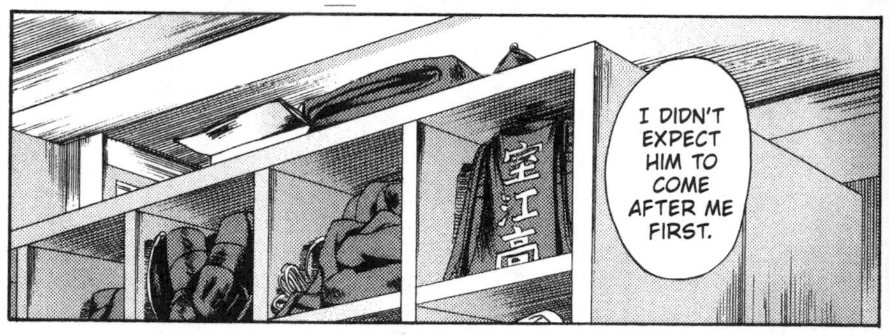
室江高
I DIDN'T EXPECT HIM TO COME AFTER ME FIRST.

TOYAMA-KUN, YOU MEAN? HA-HA, I KNOW!
BUT HE LOVES TO PICK ON OTHERS. HE'S THE BEST ON THE TEAM.

HE LIKES TO BEAT DOWN THE NEW MEMBERS FIRST...
...SO HE CAN ESTABLISH HIS SUPERIORITY RIGHT OFF THE BAT.

EVEN THE GIRLS?
OH YEAH!
BOYS OR GIRLS, IT DOESN'T MATTER TO HIM!

IN FACT, I THINK HE PICKS ON THE GIRLS EVEN MORE!
HE'S ONE SADISTIC PUPPY, I CAN TELL YOU THAT!

YOU KNOW HOW IT IS IN THE CO-ED SPORTS CLUBS!
THE GUYS JUST HAVE TO SHOW OFF AND ACT BIG!!

AND THERE'S A CERTAIN TYPE OF APE AMONG THEM...
...WHO FINDS CLUB TIME TO BE THE BEST PLACE TO EXPRESS HIS DOMI-NANCE!!

SALLY FORTH, TAMA-CHAN!! DESTROY THE GREATEST EVIL THIS CLUB HAS EVER PRODUCED!!
TEACH TOYAMA-KUN A LESSON AND MAKE HIM STOP HARASSING AND LORDING IT OVER THE REST OF US!!!

UM, KIRI-NO-SAN?
YES?

DO YOU HAVE ANY OTH-ER HAKA-MAS?

THIS ONE DOESN'T FIT...
BUKA (FLOP)
BUKA

BUT THAT'S THE SMALL-EST ONE WE HAVE...
I'M SORRY. I'M REALLY SMALL.

HRRM! CAN'T FIND ANY! OH DEAR.
GASA GOSO (THWOP SHFF)
YOU'LL STEP ON THE HEM OF THAT ONE.

I CAN FOLD THE FRONT UP...

BUT NOT THE BACK. MY HEEL WILL CATCH IT.

MAYBE WE SHOULD FORGET ABOUT THIS FOR TODAY. YOU CAN BRING IN YOUR OWN TOMORROW OR SOMETHING...
NO, I'LL DO IT.

SINCE IT'S ***JUST FOR TODAY***.

む-
MUU (HMM)

ALL RIGHT, THEN.
BE CAREFUL!
I WILL.

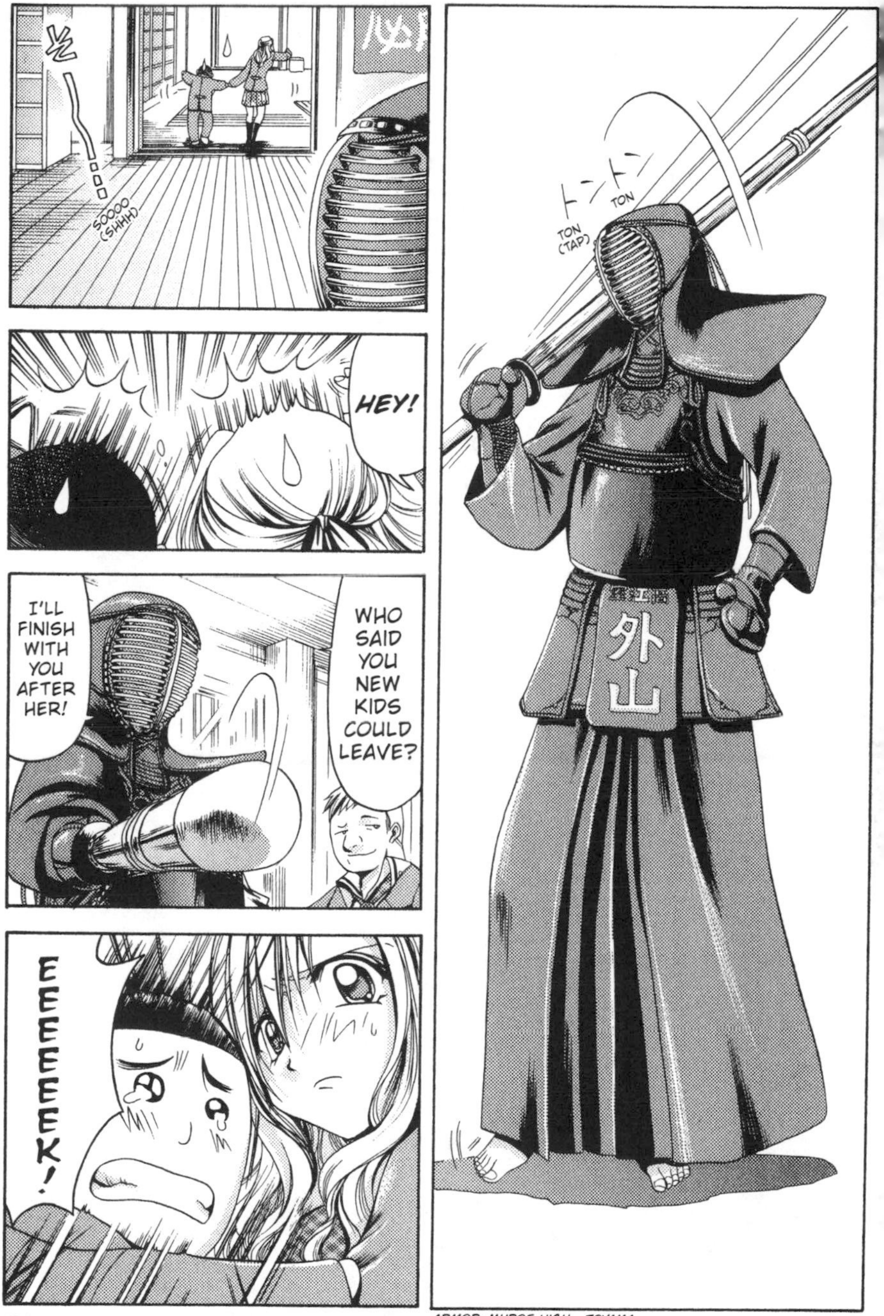

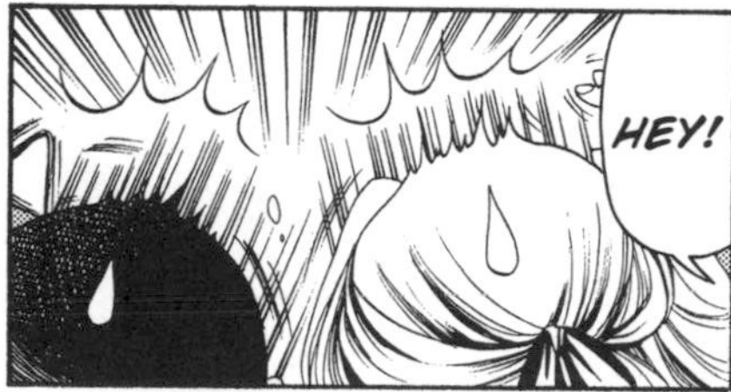

トントン
TON TON (TAP)

外山

ARMOR: MUROE HIGH - TOYAMA

室江高
ずる...
ZURU
(DRAG)

I WILL DO MY BEST FOR YOU, SIR.
TOOK YOU LONG ENOUGH.
ALL RIGHT, LET ME SEE WHATCHA GOT.
BUN (WHOOSH)
ZA (BOOM)

WATCH OUT, TOYAMA USES A CARBON SHINAI.

IT HURTS WHEN YOU GET WHACKED WITH IT. OOH, ES-PECIALLY ON THE GAUNT-LET!
YIKES!

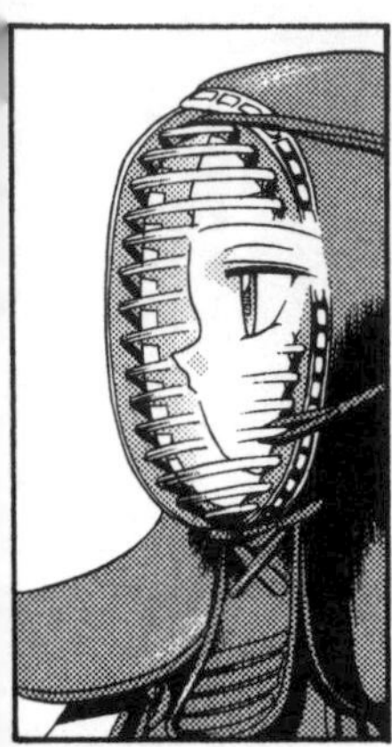

THAT'S WHY HE USES IT— BECAUSE IT'S HARDER!
SHUT YOUR TRAP, IWASA.

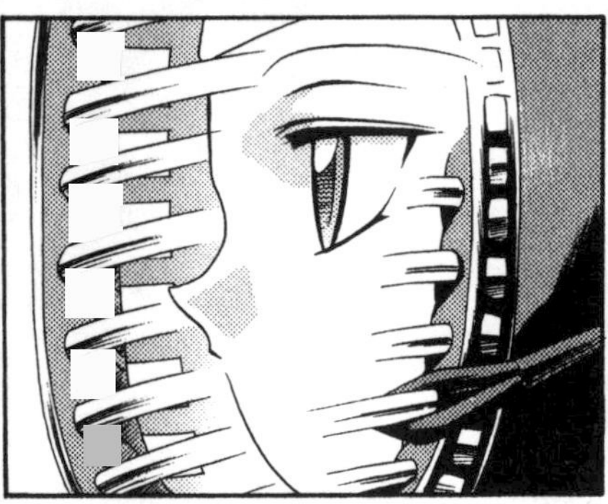

THE WORST IS HOW HE INTEN-TIONALLY AIMS FOR THE WEAK SPOT JUST OFF THE GAUNTLET, SO HE CAN WATCH THE OPPONENT SQUIRM IN PAIN!
TOYAMA'S A BAD, BAD MAN, LET ME TELL YOU THAT!

KNOCK IT OFF, IDIOT.
HA HA HA.

AND NOW THAT WE'VE GOTTEN THE WARM-UP THREATS OVER WITH...
BI (FWP)
GAKU
GAKU
GAKU (SHIVER)
...GET HIM!
DON'T LISTEN TO WHAT THAT IDIOT IWASA JUST SAID, UHH... KAWAZOE-SAN?
RELAX YOUR STANCE.
THIS ISN'T A FORMAL MATCH.
I'M NOT GONNA HURT YOU, YOU KNOW.
I MEAN ...
...IT'S JUST KENDO.

MAN, I'M LATE!
たったったっ
TA (TMP) TA TA

SIGN: MARTIAL ARTS HALL
パン
PAN (WHACK)
WHOA!
パァン
PAAN

SIGN: KENDO CLUB
剣道部
パシィ
PASHI (THWACK)
パシャ
PASHI

WOW, DO I HEAR SOME SERIOUS PRAC-TICE...?
THAT'S THE SOUND OF REAL KENDO!

AHHH, THIS TAKES ME BACK ...
じーん...
JIIIN (LAHHH)

ガラッ
GARA (SHHK)

PAAN
BISHI (BSHAKK)
BASHI (THAKK)
TAMA-CHAN?
BO (WHOM)
BASHI
GO (THDD)
BASHIN (THWACK)
BI (TKK)

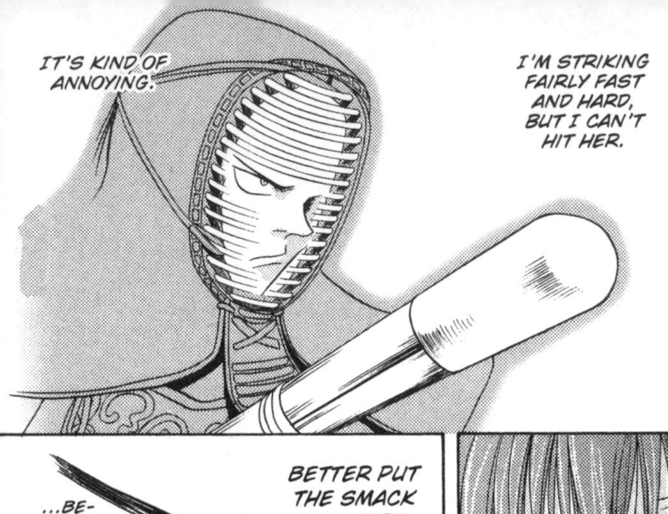

GIRI (GRRT)

DIE, BITCH!

DO (WHMM)

FUO
(FZZ)

DOU
(DOMMM)

SIGN: FACULTY ROOM

キリッ
KIRI (GRRT)

Illustration:Aguri Igarashi

Illustration: Masahiro Totsuka

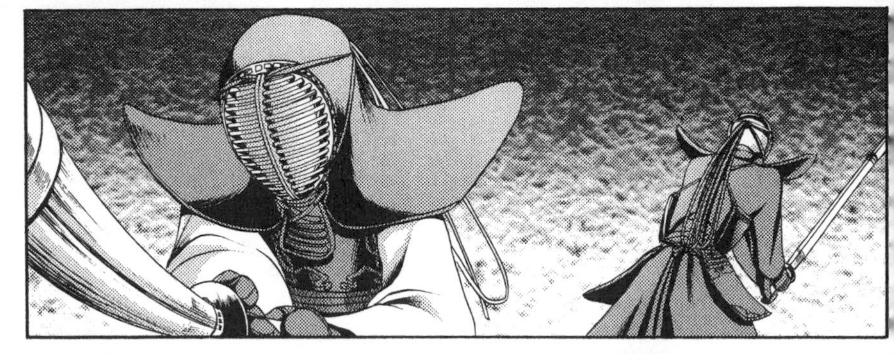

LABEL: MUROE HIGH

!
NO, TOYA-MA-KUN!
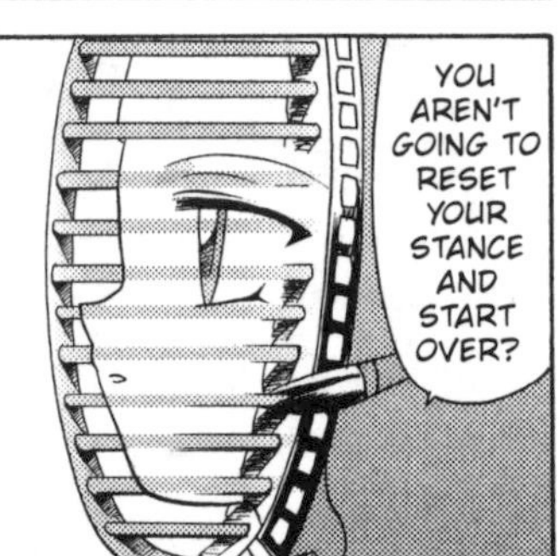
YOU AREN'T GOING TO RESET YOUR STANCE AND START OVER?
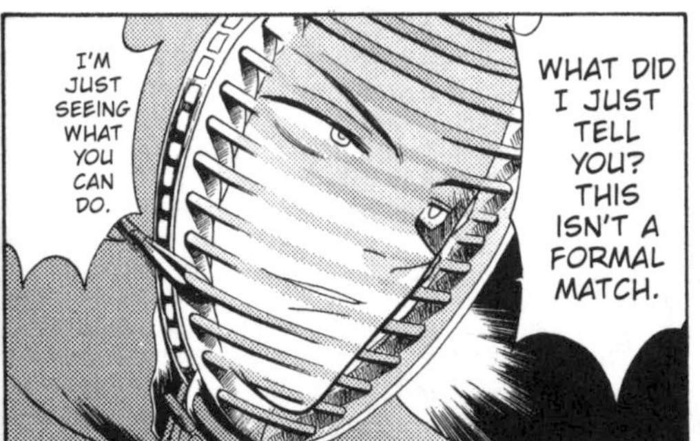
WHAT DID I JUST TELL YOU? THIS ISN'T A FORMAL MATCH.
I'M JUST SEEING WHAT YOU CAN DO.

GAA (DMM)

PAAN (WHAM)

PAAN
(WHACK)
PASHII
(SHWAKK)

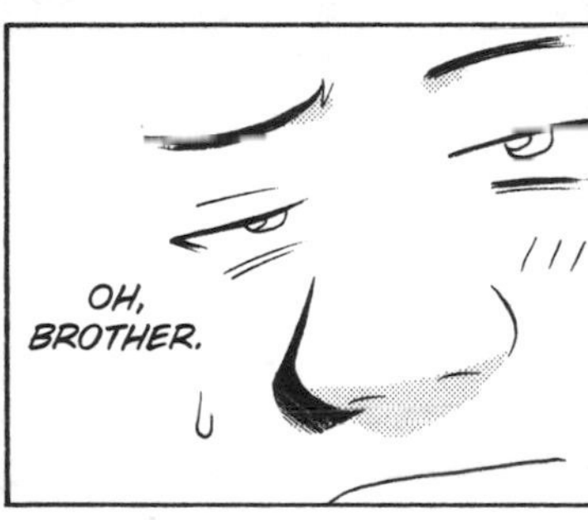
OH, BROTHER.

WHAT'S HER NAME...TAMAKI KAWAZOE? POOR THING...SHE LOOKS FAIRLY GOOD AT THIS STUFF...
PAN
(WHACK)
PASHI
(THWACK)

SHE PROBABLY SAW TOYAMA ACTING TOUGH AND DECIDED SHE WANTED TO TEACH HIM A LESSON.
IF ONLY SHE'D KNOWN BETTER. IT'S NOT LIKE A MATCH, WHERE YOU GET ONE OR TWO GOOD HITS IN AND YOU WIN.

TOYAMA DOESN'T CARE ABOUT KENDO ITSELF.
HE JUST WANTS TO BEAT THE CRAP OUT OF HIS OPPONENT.

HE'S ONE SADISTIC PUPPY.

CHAPTER 7
TOYAMA AND HIS PRIDE

KENDO IS...

SIGN: SIMPLE, HONEST, STRONG, UPRIGHT

IT IS THE LEARNING OF THE WARRIOR'S MINDSET THROUGH THE WAYS OF THE SWORD THAT IS MOST CRUCIAL OF ALL.

UNLIKE THE BATTLES THAT WARRIORS FOUGHT WITH REAL KATANAS, IT IS CONDUCTED IN MODERN TIMES AS A TOOL OF SELF-BETTERMENT, PRIMARILY AS A STUDENT ACTIVITY.

...A MEANS OF DISCIPLINING ONE'S MIND THROUGH RIGOROUS PHYSICAL TRAINING.

LISTEN TO ME, TAMAKI.
THE GOAL OF KENDO IS NOT TO CUT DOWN THE OPPONENT.

THE JAPANESE KATANA IS MADE TO SLICE CLEANLY THROUGH THE TARGET.
YOU CAN CLEARLY SEE WHERE THIS DIFFERS FROM KENDO.

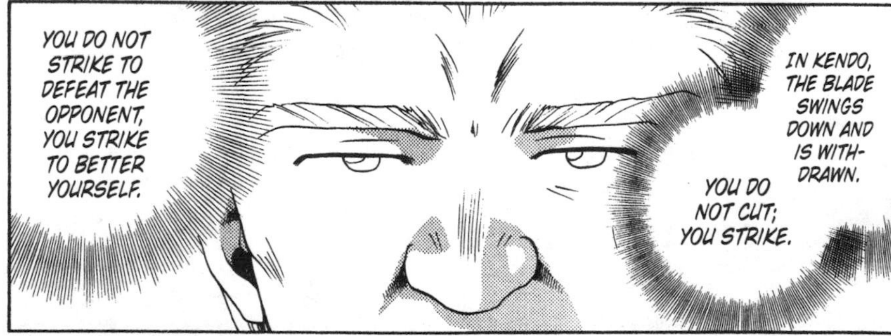

IN KENDO, THE BLADE SWINGS DOWN AND IS WITHDRAWN.
YOU DO NOT CUT; YOU STRIKE.
YOU DO NOT STRIKE TO DEFEAT THE OPPONENT, YOU STRIKE TO BETTER YOURSELF.

TAMA-CHAN, AGE 4.

......

SORRY.

THIS WAS TOO SOON.

BUT YOU MUST UNDERSTAND THIS, TAMAKI.
KENDO BEGINS AND ENDS WITH AN EXPRESSION OF GRATITUDE.

IT IS A SPORT THAT DEMANDS MANNERS ABOVE ALL ELSE.
THERE'S NOTHING TO BE AFRAID OF.

NOW...
...PICK UP THE SHINAI.
BASHI (WHAMM)
ZA... (SSUP)
WHAT'S WRONG WITH YOU?
COME AFTER ME, KAWAZOE-SAN!
BIRI (BRR) ビリビリ BIRI
DA!! (DMM)
IT'S NOT A MATCH?
THEN THIS ISN'T KENDO.

HENN!!
PAAN
(WHAAK)
外山
PAAN

TAA!
BO (WHOKK)
LABEL: MUROE HIGH—TOYAMA

HAH!!
BAAN (WHAMM)

コオオ…
KOO...
(KSHH...)

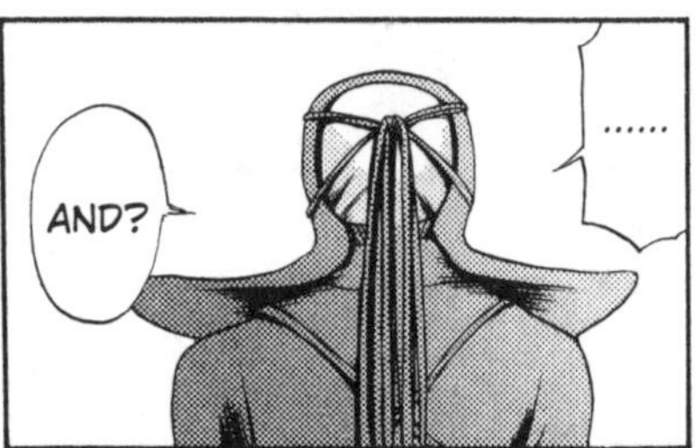
......
AND?

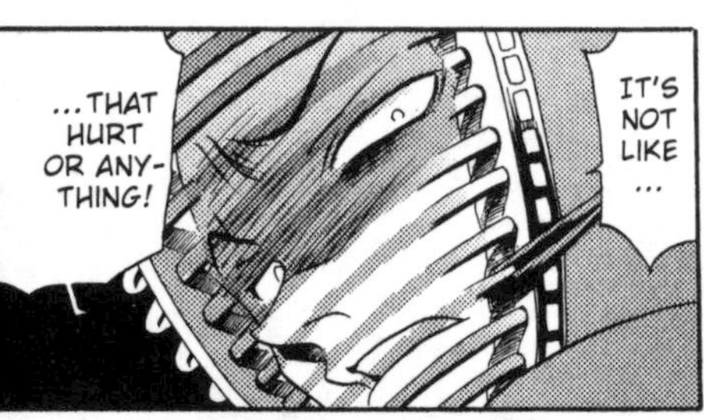
IT'S NOT LIKE ...
...THAT HURT OR ANY-THING!

BASHI
(FWACK)

I CAN TELL YOU'VE DONE THIS A LOT.
I GUESS I WOULDN'T STAND A CHANCE IN A REAL MATCH!

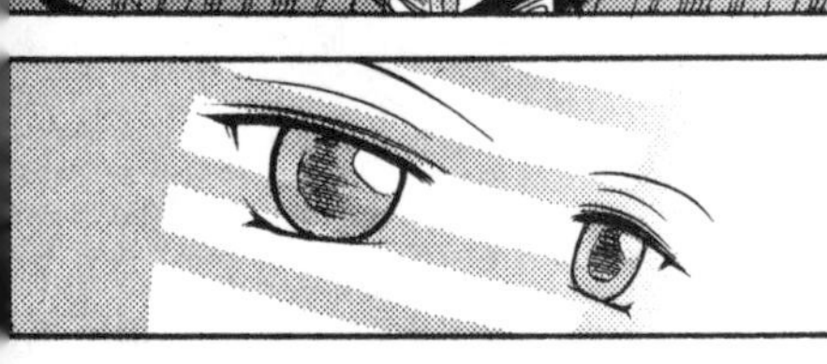

BUT YOU'RE TOO WEAK TO HURT ME!
YOUR LITTLE SWATS ARE LIKE PATS ON THE HEAD!

THINGS LOOK BAD.

GIVE IT UP, TOYAMA. YOU PICKED THE WRONG OPPONENT.

YOUR USUAL RULE-IGNORING, OVERPOWERING STRATEGY ISN'T EVEN WORKING ON THIS KID.

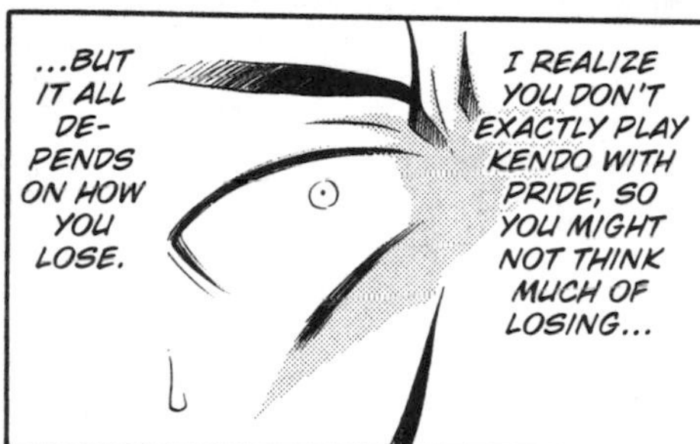
I REALIZE YOU DON'T EXACTLY PLAY KENDO WITH PRIDE, SO YOU MIGHT NOT THINK MUCH OF LOSING...
...BUT IT ALL DEPENDS ON HOW YOU LOSE.

AND THIS TAMAKI KAWAZOE...
...IS BAD NEWS, MAN.

YOU JUST GOT SMACKED AROUND BY A GIRL—A GIRL FAR TINIER AND YOUNGER THAN YOU.

I CAN TELL YOU'RE GETTING MAD NOW.

NOT ONLY THAT, YOU GOT HIT IN THE FACE THREE TIMES...WITH SUCH AN EXTREME DIFFERENCE IN HEIGHT!
I DON'T BELIEVE IT MYSELF.

SHE HIT YOU THREE STRAIGHT TIMES TO CHIDE YOU FOR NOT STRAIGHTENING UP AND STARTING OVER.
I CAN'T EVEN FATHOM HOW GOOD THIS TAMAKI KAWAZOE MUST BE...

DO
(BOOM)

GU
(GRRK)

!

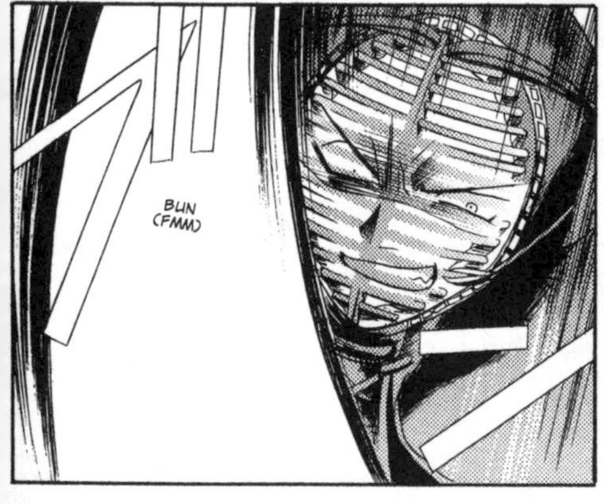

PAAN
(WHAM)

HUH? TAMA-CHAN JUST FELL OVER.
I WAS AFRAID OF THAT...

?
WE DIDN'T HAVE ANY HAKAMAS IN HER SIZE, SO SHE STEPPED ON THE HEM.

AHH, I SEE.
NO WONDER HER MOVE-MENTS ARE AWKWARD.

YAH!!
PAAN
(WHACK)
YAH!!
PAN
YAH!!

GU (GRRK)

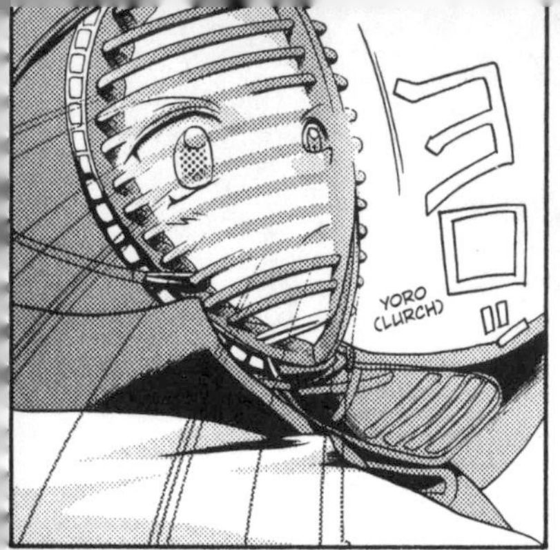
YORO (LURCH)

SHA!
SHA!
BASHI (FWAPP)
BASHII

AU AU (AAH EEP)
あう あう
HE'S PRESSING WITH FULL FORCE NOW.
THIS LOOKS BAD...
NOT QUITE...

IT'S NOT AS MUCH OF A HANDICAP AS YOU THINK.

SUPAAN (THWAM)

ABEL: MUROE HIGH - TOYAMA

OH, COME ON NOW... WE GOTTA STOP THIS THING.
BUT HOW TO BRING IT TO AN END?
TOYA-MA'S PUTTING HIMSELF RIGHT WHERE SHE WANTS HIM.
HE ISN'T CONNECT-ING ONCE... HIS OVER-POWERING STRATEGY IS BACK-FIRING.

SHE'S WAY BEYOND HIS LEVEL.
IF HE WON'T ADMIT DEFEAT AND WON'T LAND A SINGLE HIT, THIS WILL NEVER END.
JUST LET HIM HIT YOU AND LOSE ON PURPOSE, TAMAKI KAWAZOE.
THIS IS GETTING RIDICULOUS.

ARE YOU REALLY GONNA KEEP THIS UP UNTIL SOMEONE RUNS OUT OF STRENGTH AND CAN'T MOVE ANYMORE, TOYAMA!?
EVERY SECOND THIS DRAGS ON, THE MORE PITIFUL YOU BECOME! JUST CALL IT OFF!

ZA
(SHFF)

TIME TO PUT THIS SUCKER IN ACTION!
I SURE HOPE TOYAMA AND IWASA HELP OUT WITH THIS.
BYE, SEN-SEI!

I BET THEY'LL AGREE IF I OFFER TO HELP CLEAN UP THEIR STUDENT RECORDS.
HELL, THEY MIGHT BE GUNG HO ON THE WHOLE DEAL!
シナリオ

LABEL: SCENARIO

SCENE (1)
"TWO BOYS ATTACK THE KENDO CLUB OUT OF NOWHERE. IN FACT, THEY ARE DELINQUENTS AND FORMER MEMBERS OF THE CLUB."
I MEAN, IT FITS THEM TO A "T."
AND THEY'RE DOING THIS BECAUSE... LET'S SAY SOMEONE IN THE CLUB GAVE THEM A REASON TO BE ANGRY.

EIGA'S PERFECT FOR GETTING IN TROUBLE.
SAY HE STEPS ON THEIR SHOES OR SPILLS JUICE ON THEM.

SCENE (2)
"THE KENDO CLUB IS CRUSHED BY THE TWO DELINQUENTS. NONE AMONG THEM CAN WITHSTAND THEIR OVERPOWERING STRENGTH."

THESE TWO CAN HELP PLAY ALONG WITH THAT PART.
AND THEN COMES THE APPEARANCE OF OUR HERO!! TAMAKI KAWAZOE!!
A STEADFAST FAN OF COSTUMED HEROES, SHE WILL LET NO BAD DEED GO UNPUNISHED!!

THIS IS BRILLIANT! FAILPROOF!
ふははははは
FU-HA-HA-HA-HA
ONCE SHE PICKS UP A SHINAI, IT'S ALL IN THE BAG!
HE'S ALWAYS STOKED ON SOMETHING.
WHAT'S UP, SENSEI?

THE ONLY QUESTION IS, WHICH OF THE TWO IS MORE SUITED FOR THE VILLAIN?
TOYAMA COULD PROBABLY JUST ACT AS HIMSELF AND FIT THE PART.

HE IS SADISTIC, AFTER ALL.

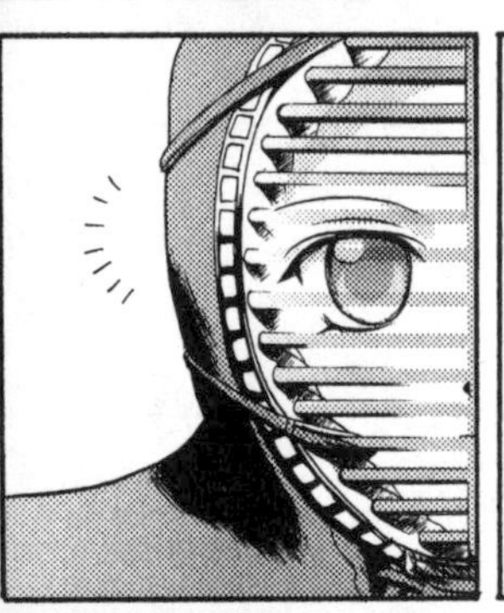

...OF COURSE...

...I CAN USE THAT...

ピッ
PI (BEEP)

ジャーーン
JAAAN (DA-DAAA)

ジャジャジャ ドンパンドンパン
JA JA JA DONPAN DONPAN (DA-DA-DA BOOM-BAP BOOM-BAP)
超剣戦隊
SUPER SWORD SQUAD
ブレードブレイバー®
BLADE BRAVER
BAAAN (BAMMM)

Blade Braverrrr !!
ジャーン
JAAAN

We have to stop Death Armor from taking over the world!!
Yeah!!

The town's under attack! You're gonna get it, Death Armor!!
Bwa-ha-ha-ha-ha-ha-ha-ha!!
WAAA (GRM-MM)
ワァァァ

Foolish Blade Bravers! Your powers are no match for mine!!
I am the greatest! This world belongs to me!!

You won't get away with this, Death Armor!!
We're gonna take you down and save the world!!

CHAPTER 8
TAMAKI AND BLADE BRAVER

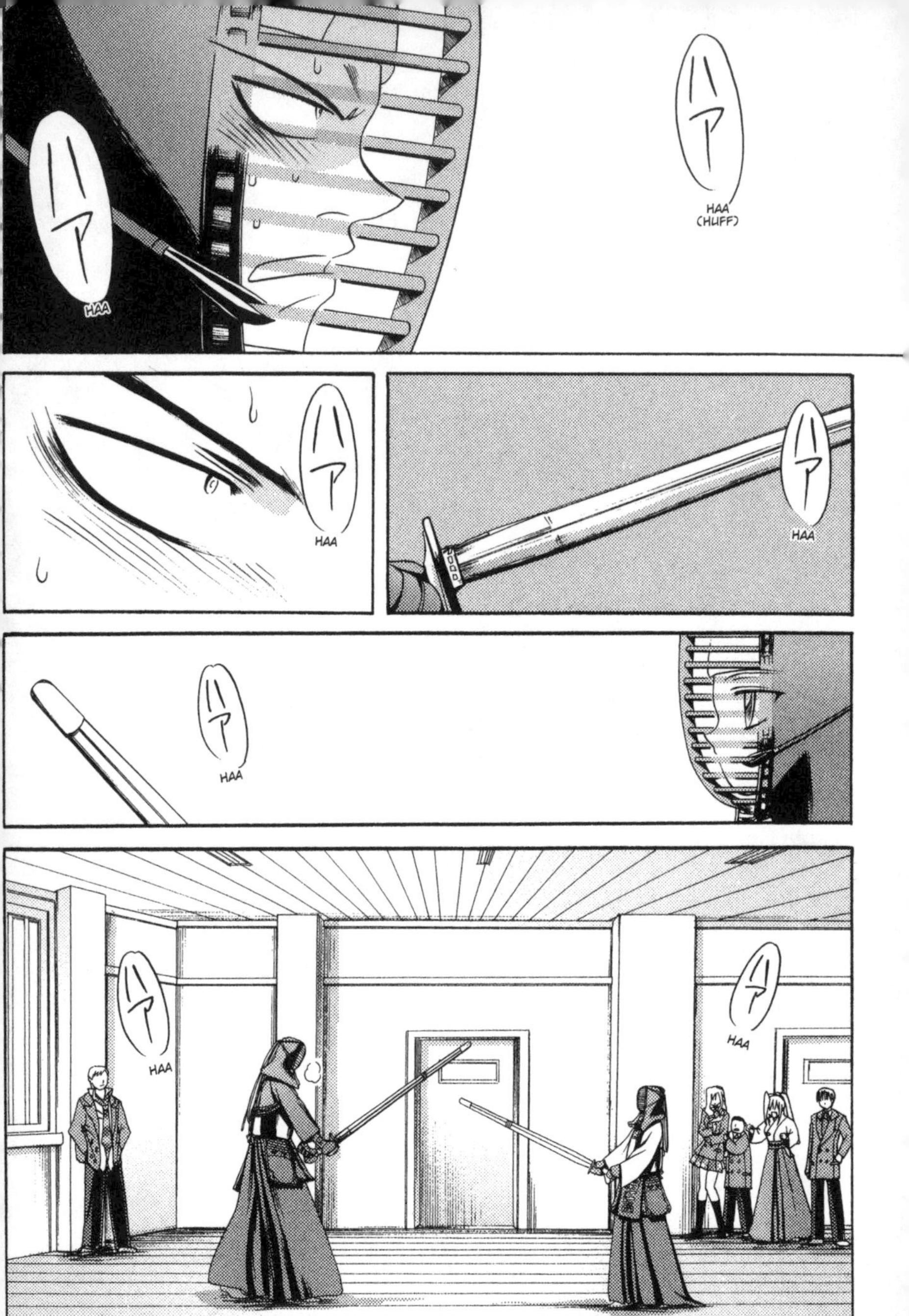

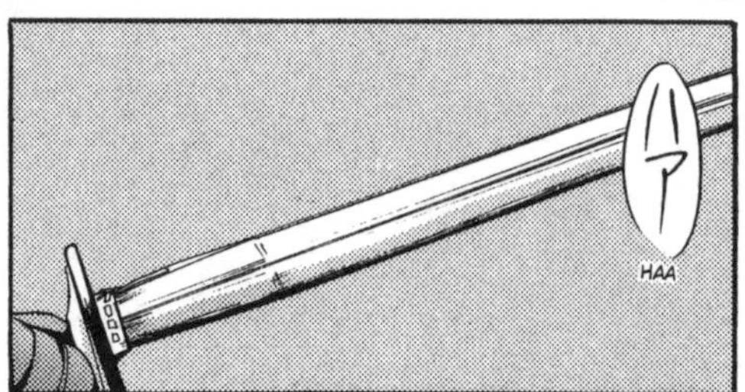

ハア
HAA

ハア
HAA

HOW LONG IS THIS GOING TO LAST? I'VE NEVER SEEN A KENDO MATCH GO SO LONG...
SHOULD I JUST STEP IN AND GO, "OKAY, TIME'S UP"?

HELL NO. WITH TOYAMA THIS FURIOUS, THERE'S NO WAY I CAN STOP THINGS AS THEY ARE NOW. HE'D GO NUTS ON ME AFTERWARD...
I'M SCARED OF WHAT WOULD HAPPEN TO ME...

LABEL: TOYAMA

CAPTAIN KIRINO, WE SHOULD PROBABLY STOP THIS SOON...
RIGHT...

FOR HIS SAKE.

RIGHT ...

TAMA-CHAN, TOYAMA-KUN, GOOD MATCH ALL AROUND!
OKAY, OKAY, OKAY, OKAY, OKAY!
BOY, IT'S HOT IN HERE! YOU MUST BE TIRED!
クーラー BOX

LABEL: COOLER

LET'S ALL SIT DOWN AND CRACK OPEN SOME DRINKS!
HERE'S SOME DELICIOUS SHISO JUICE! IT WORKS GREAT ON THOSE POLLEN ALLERGIES!!
ENIENI
しそ
しそパワーで花粉もコワくない!
果汁20%

JUICE BOX: A GOOD SOURCE OF NUTRIENTS! / SHISO DRINK / STOP WORRYING ABOUT FLOWER POLLEN TODAY! / 20% FRUIT JUICE

......
CAN I HAVE IT, THEN?
I'LL FINISH HER WITH THE NEXT ONE.

SHE CAN'T PULL BACK, BECAUSE HER HAKAMA IS TOO BIG.
SO I'LL PUSH AND PUSH AND PUSH UNTIL SHE'S FORCED TO GIVE WAY AND I CAN THRASH HER!

SHE CAN PECK AND NIP AT ME ALL SHE WANTS.
IN THE END, SHE CAN'T MATCH A MAN IN SHEER STRENGTH!

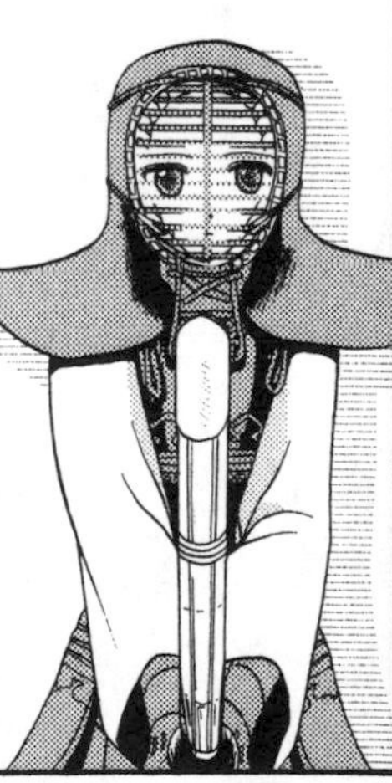
IF NONE OF MY HITS ARE GOING TO AFFECT HIM...

LISTEN TO ME, TAMAKI.
YOU MUST NOT THRUST.

YOU PUT TOO MUCH STRENGTH IN YOUR THRUSTS.
YOU LUNGE AS IF YOU ARE DEFEATING THE WICKED.

KEEP YOUR THRUST HIDDEN.

AGAINST EVERYONE?
YOU MAY USE IT ON ME, OF COURSE.

AND PERHAPS... ON AN OLDER MAN, IF NECES-SARY.
ONLY ONE WITH KENDO EXPERI-ENCE.

AND ONLY ONCE YOU ARE IN HIGH SCHOOL.
UNDER-STAND? OTHER-WISE, IT'S TOO DAN-GEROUS.

...BUT WHY? WHAT MAKES MY THRUSTS SO DANGEROUS...?

DOU (DMMM)

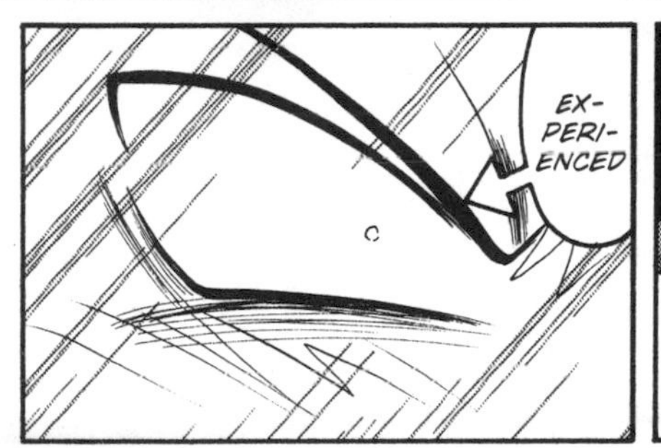

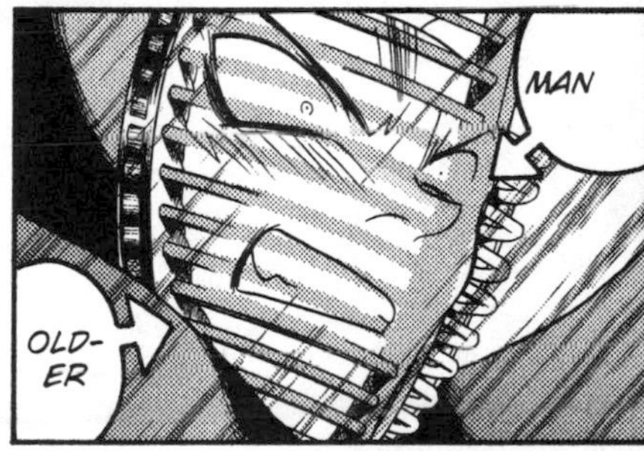

AND
I'M...

...IN HIGH
SCHOOL
NOW.

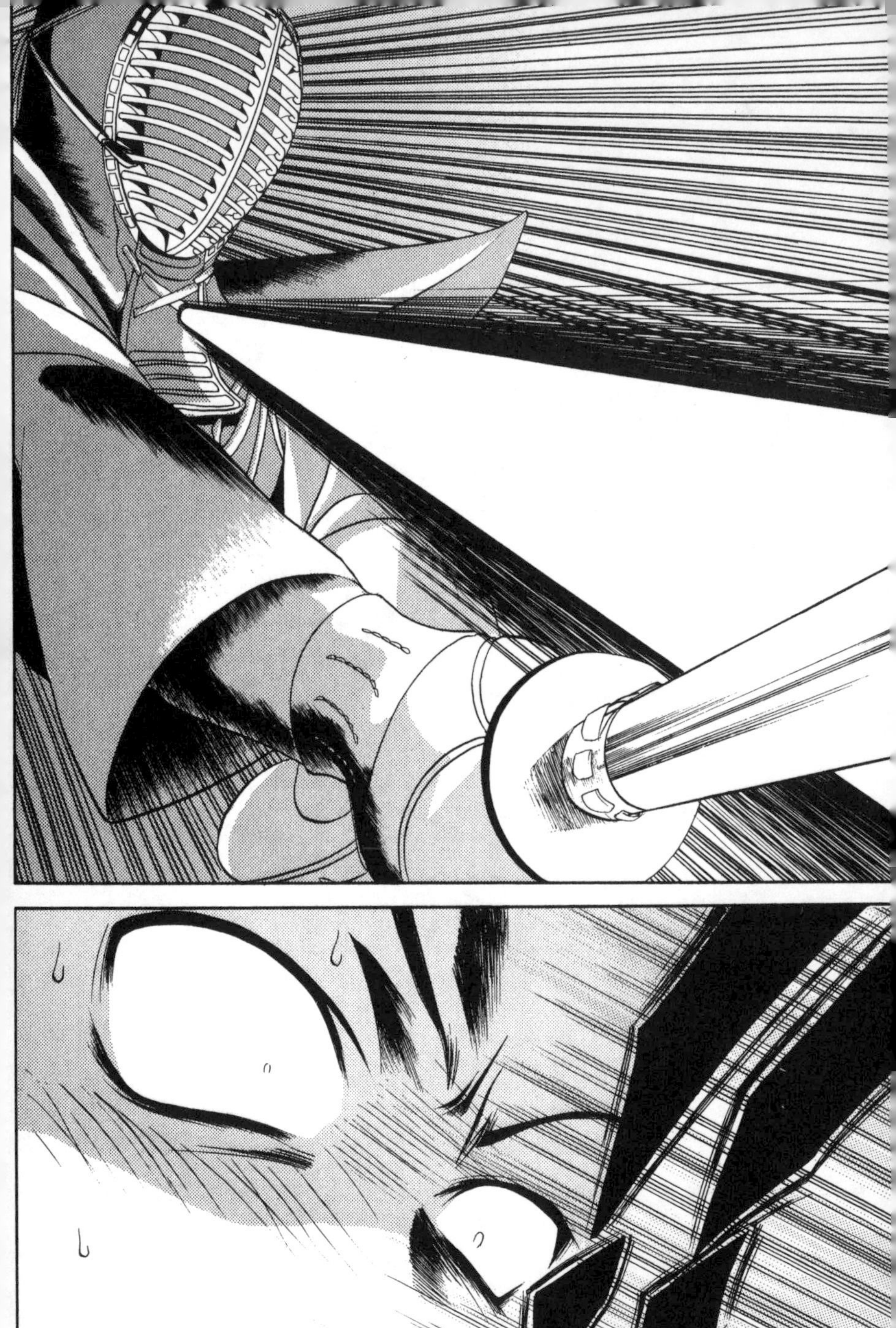

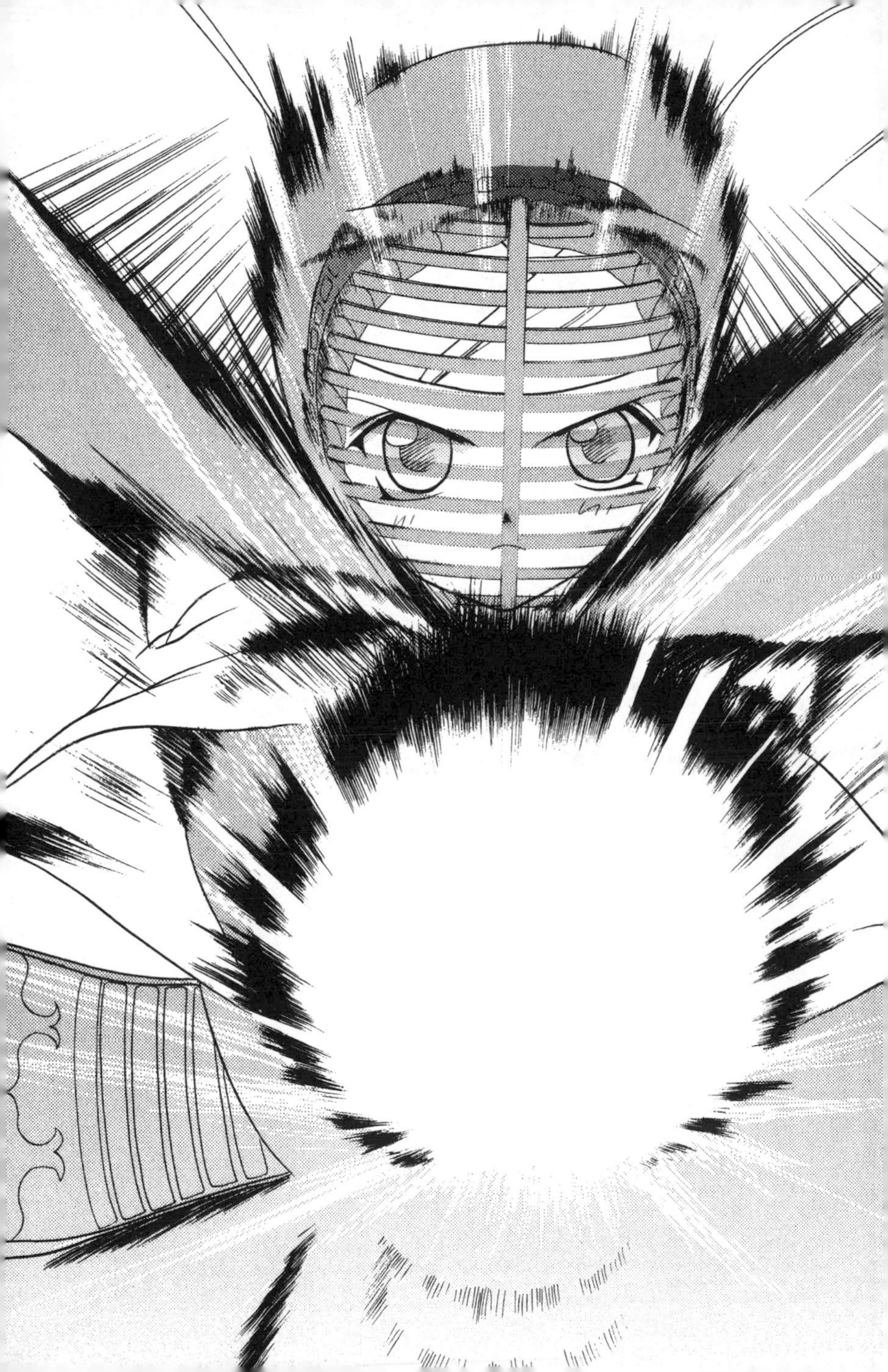

ZUZA (SKSHH)
Aaaagh!

Bwa-ha-ha! Did you think you could stop me!!?
Shoot! He's too strong!

Take this!!

That won't work on me!!
Aaaahh!!

DOSA (THWUD)
No! Guys!!

I'm not down and out yet!

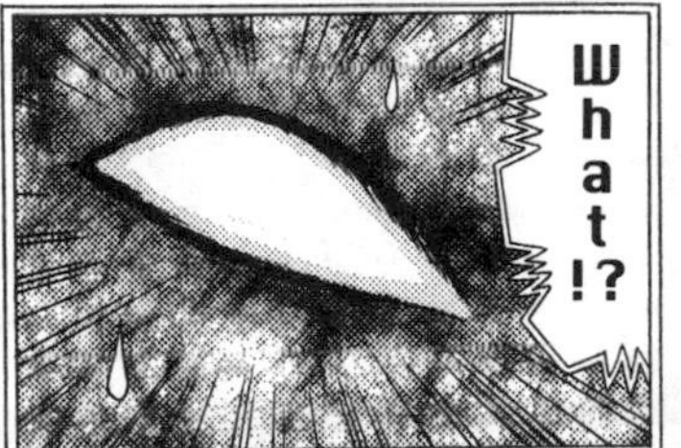

Atomic Fire Blade !!!

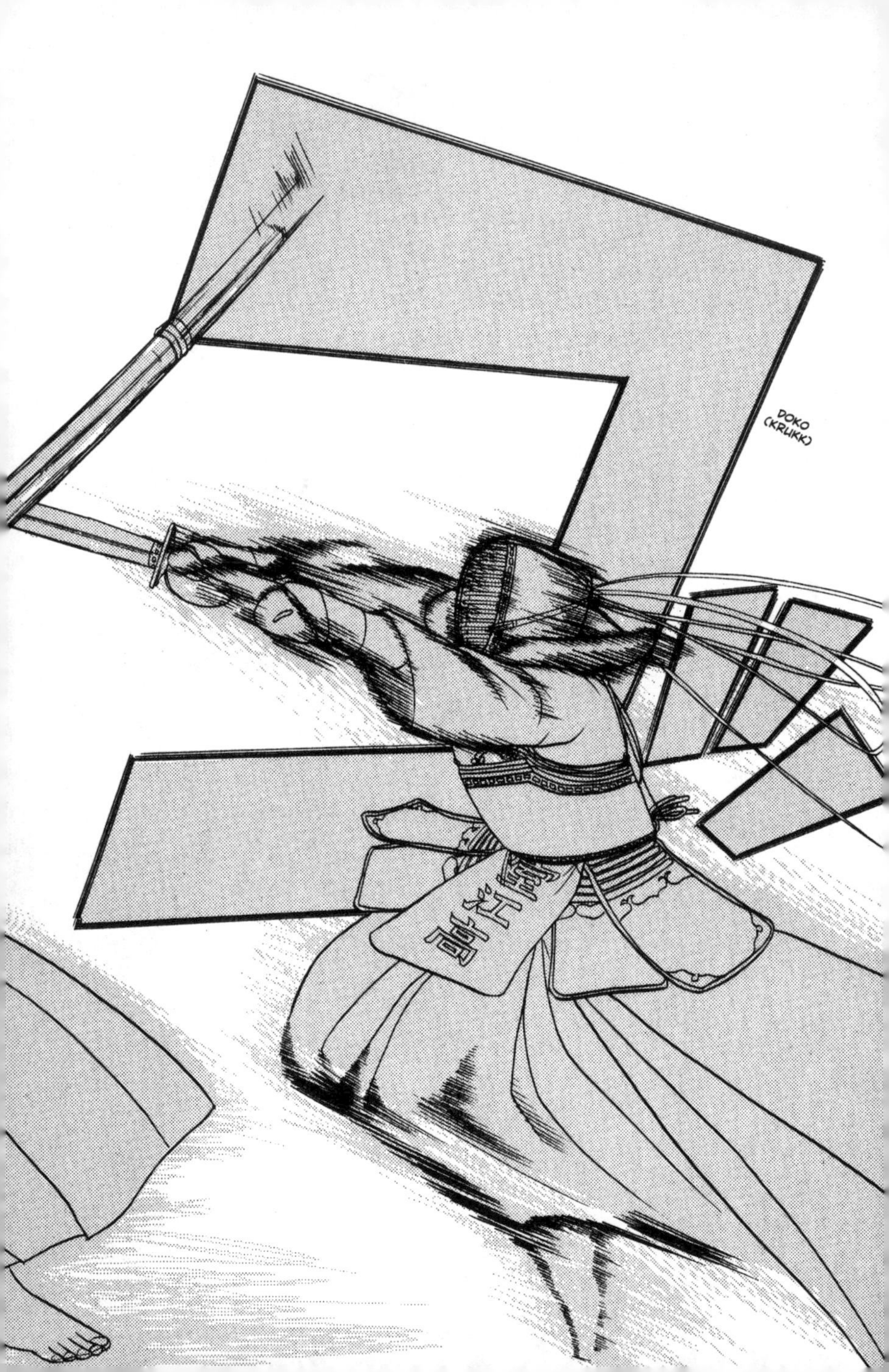
DOKO
(KRUKK)
室江高

ドオン
DOON
(DOOMM)

GARA (SHUNK)

HUH?

UH...

...

DAMN, TOYAMA, YOU JUST LOST, MAN!! HA-HA-HA!
WHAT HAP-PENED? DID YOU TRIP!? THAT WAS NUTS!

I'M HUNGRY, DUDE. LET'S JUST GO.

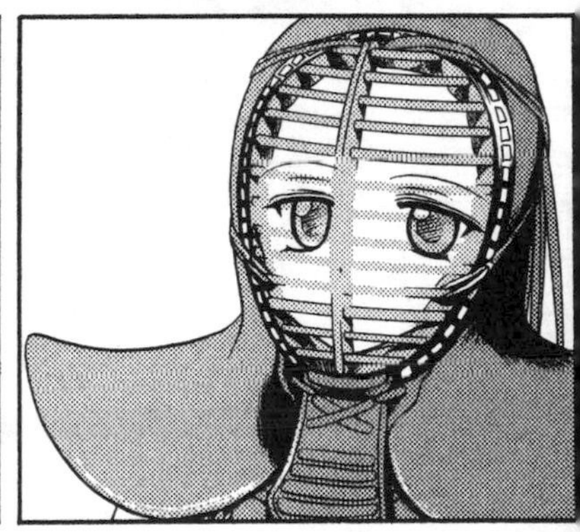

TAMA-CHAN.

?
?

COME ON!

I DON'T KNOW HOW LONG I'LL BE HERE... BUT FOR NOW, I'D LIKE TO BE IN THE CLUB.

ワァァァ

WAAAA (YAYYY)

ペコ

PEKO (BOW)

PAPER: SCENARIO

Illustration:Aguri Igarashi

Illustration:Masahiro Totsuka

チュン
CHUN (CHIRP)
チュン
CHUN

I'M LEAVING FOR SCHOOL.

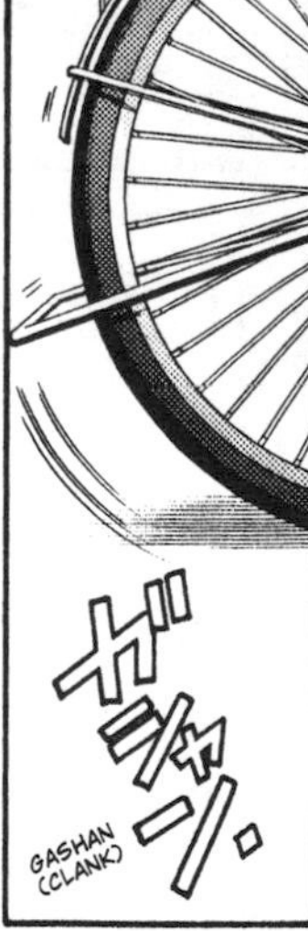
ガシャン
GASHAN (CLANK)

TA-MA-KI.
IS THAT ...?

WHAT?

OH ...
I JOINED THE KENDO CLUB.

SEE YOU WHEN I GET HOME.
CHIRIRIN (RING)
WAIT!

I SEE ...

WELL, EITHER SHE MADE SOME FRIENDS OR WAS CONVINCED BY HER TEACHER ...
...BUT AT ANY RATE, I'M GLAD SHE GOT IN THE MOOD.

KI (SCR-RCH)

NO...

CHAPTER 9
KOJIRO AND THE DAY HE GAVE UP THE SHINAI OF HIS HEART
I JOINED TO HELP SAVE THE CLUB FROM EVIL.
... PAR-DON?

WAI WAI
(WHEE)

職員室

SIGN: FACULTY ROOM

GOOD MORN-ING!
ZAWA ZAWA
(MURMUR)
PŪRURURURU
(RING)
MORN-ING.
2-4

CAN YOU WAIT A LITTLE BIT, SENPAI?
PLEASE!
I DON'T HAVE ENOUGH MEM-BERS YET...
YEAH.

BY NEXT MONTH FOR SURE.
THEN WE'LL HAVE OUR MATCH!!

ギシ
GISHI (CRRK)
HRRRM.

...THAT'S THE PROB-LEM.

I STILL NEED ONE MORE.

TAMAKI KAWAZOE.
KIRINO CHIBA.
MIYAKO MIYAZAKI.

AND THEN SAYAKO KUWAHARA... THAT'S ONLY FOUR.
BUT WE HAVEN'T HAD SAYA IN THE DOJO ONCE.

I'LL HAVE TO MAKE KIRINO DRAG SAYA IN HERE, ONE WAY OR ANOTHER ...
THEN ONE MORE... AND I'LL NEED SOMEONE WITH KENDO EXPERI-ENCE.

AS-SUM-ING TAMA WILL WIN ONE...
AND KIRINO AND SAYA MIGHT MANAGE ONE WIN BETWEEN THEM...
MIYA-MIYA... NOT GONNA HAPPEN.

NEED ONE MORE WIN...
ONE MORE PLAYER CAPABLE OF WIN-NING...

ONE MORE...

HEY, HOW HARD CAN IT BE TO FIND ONE MORE PERSON!!?
NO SWEAT!

IT'D BE A BETTER USE OF MY TIME TO TRAIN UP THE GIRLS I'VE ALREADY GOT!!
OKAY, LET'S GET A TRAINING MENU DRAWN UP!!

LOOK AT YOU, ISHIDA-SENSEI.
YOU'RE REALLY EXCITED ABOUT THIS PRACTICE MEET.

SORRY ABOUT THE NOISE, YOSHI-KAWA-SENSEI!
IT'S ALL RIGHT.

NOR-MALLY, YOU SEEM REALLY OUT OF IT...
I WAS WORRIED THAT YOU MIGHT BE HAVING PROBLEMS.
UM, OH.

TEACH-ERS AND STU-DENTS SEEM KIND OF DULL AND TIRED THESE DAYS.
THERE'S NOTHING LIKE AN ENTHUSI-ASTIC, SORT OF DIM-WITTED TEACHER TO SHAKE THINGS UP!
OH, REALLY?

YES, REALLY!
HANG IN THERE, ISHI-DA-SEN-SEI!!

WHO CARES IF YOUR STU-DENTS GET A LITTLE FREAKED OUT AT FIRST?
YOU JUST KEEP PULL-ING THEM IN THE RIGHT DIRECTION, AND EVERY-THING WILL WORK OUT!

...

I DON'T THINK I CAN TELL HER WHY I'M REALLY DOING THIS...

剣道部
SIGN: KENDO CLUB

KIRINO!! HOW MANY TIMES DO I HAVE TO TELL YOU? DON'T JUST USE YOUR WRISTS WHEN YOU STRIKE!!
必勝
SIGN: VICTORY

IT LOOKS LIKE SHE'S MADE A HABIT OUT OF IT.
YEP, AND SHE'S NEVER BEEN ABLE TO CORRECT HERSELF.

YES, SIR. I'M SORRY, SIR.

TAMA!! SHOW HER THE PROPER WAY TO DO IT!
YES, SIR.
BISHU' (SHWAP)
タマ
BISHU
ARMOR: TAMA

JIIIN (WAAAH)
Ahh... With more people in here, it's like we're finally a real kendo club...
Dripping sweat... Gushing sweat... Flying sweat... Glis-tening sweat...
THERE'S MORE TO IT THAN SWEAT!!

NOW, ONE MORE TIME!!

THE TIP OF YOUR BLADE IS STAND-ING!
YOU'RE STRAIN-ING YOUR SHOUL-DERS TOO MUCH!
BUN (WHOOSH)
YES, SIRRR!

COME ON, RELAX YOUR SHOUL-DERS.
MOMI (RUB) MOMI
AHH, THAT FEELS GOOD.

ANOTHER EXAMPLE, TAMA!
YES, SIR.
BISHU
BISHU

OH, YUJI. ARE YOU SURE DAN AND MIYA-MIYA ARE OUT RUN-NING?
MOMI MOMI
AHH, THAT'S THE STUFF.
LABEL: CHIBA
YES, THEY'RE RUNNING LAPS AROUND THE SCHOOL.

THEY AREN'T READY TO WEAR GUARDS YET.

WAIT, MIYA-MIYAAA!

KIRA KIRA (SPARKLE)

I ALREADY LAPPED YOU, DAN-KUN!

KIRA

...PLUS, THEY'RE REALLY OBNOXIOUS TO HAVE HANGING AROUND.

...GOOD POINT.

YUJI, YOU SPAR WITH KIRINO.
I'M AFRAID THE BOYS' TRAINING WILL HAVE TO COME AFTER THE GIRLS' MEET IS OVER.

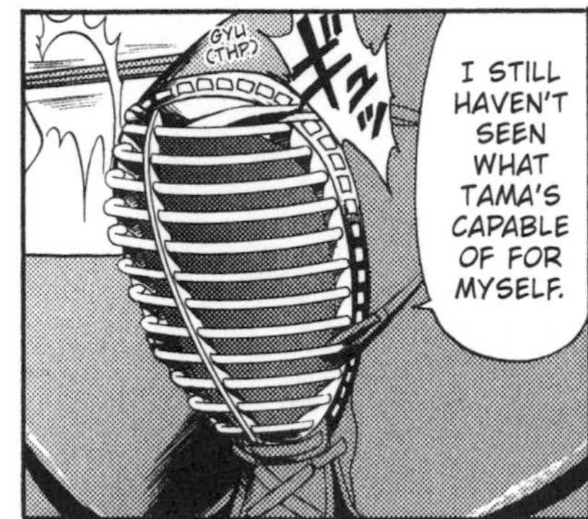
I STILL HAVEN'T SEEN WHAT TAMA'S CAPABLE OF FOR MYSELF.
GYU (THP)

GIVE ME EVERYTHING YOU'VE GOT!!
MY BODY WILL BE THE JUDGE OF WHAT YOU CAN DO!!

ARMOR: ISHIDA

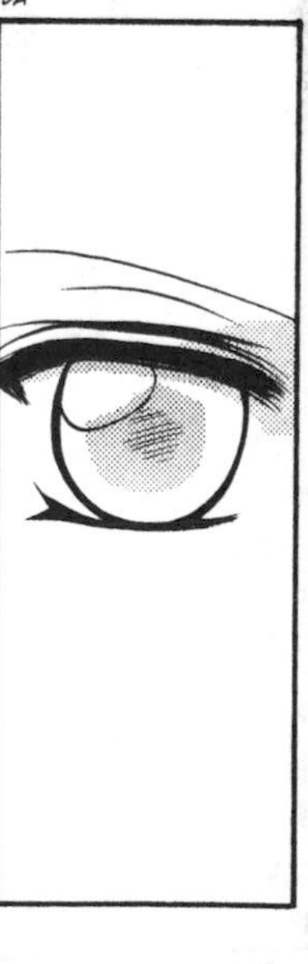

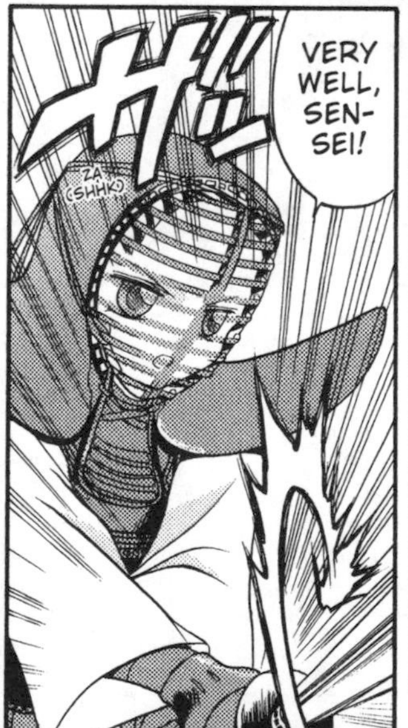
VERY WELL, SEN-SEI!
ZA (SHHK)

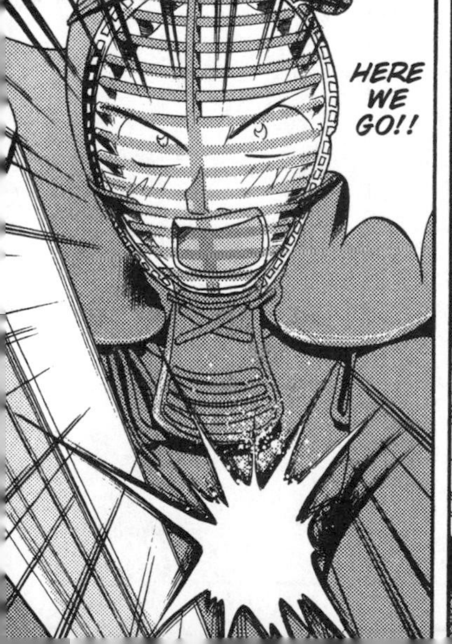
HERE WE GO!!

めん
MEN (YAH)

ぴーちく
PIIICHIKU (TWEEET)

しくしくしくしくしくしくしくしく
SHIKU (SOB) SHIKU SHIKU SHIKU SHIKU
SHIKU SHIKU SHIKU SHIKU

YOU SHOULDN'T DO THAT, TAMA-CHAN!
NO!
YEAH, SENSEI STILL HAS HIS PRIDE TO UPHOLD.

EVEN IF YOU WIN, YOU HAVE TO SHOW HIM YOU HAD A HARD TIME.
YEAH, DON'T JUST KNOCK HIM OUT IN TWO SECONDS...
EXACTLY... THAT'S JUST MEAN, WHUPPING HIM LIKE THAT.

ジャブ
ジャブ
JABU (SPOSH) JABU
SIGH...

I'VE LOST MY EDGE...

IT'S BEEN SO LONG SINCE I REALLY SWUNG A SHINAI...

HOW LONG ...?

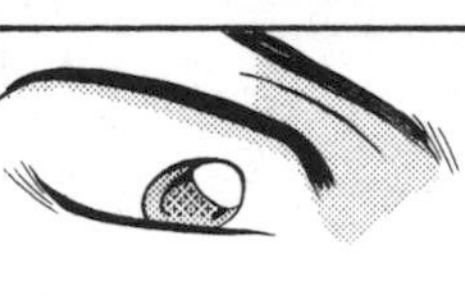
WHEN WAS THE LAST TIME...?

(AGE 18)
MY NAME IS ISHIDA! IT'S NICE TO MEET YOU!!
石田

NAME TAG: ISHIDA

I HAD JUST STARTED COLLEGE AND WAS LIVING ON MY OWN...
SO I STARTED WORKING NIGHT SHIFTS AT A MINI MART.
HEY, YOU'VE GOT SPUNK!
8 マート

SIGN: 8 MART / FRESHLY-BAKED BREAD SALE

IT'S BEEN DANGEROUS LATELY.
ESPECIALLY ON THE LATE-NIGHT SHIFT. BE CAREFUL.

LABEL: TANAKA

SIGN: NOW ON SALE

SIGN: 100 YEN SALE

OPEN THE REGISTER.

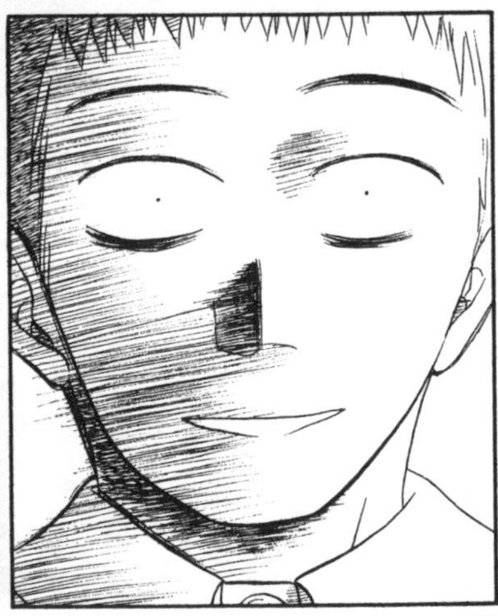

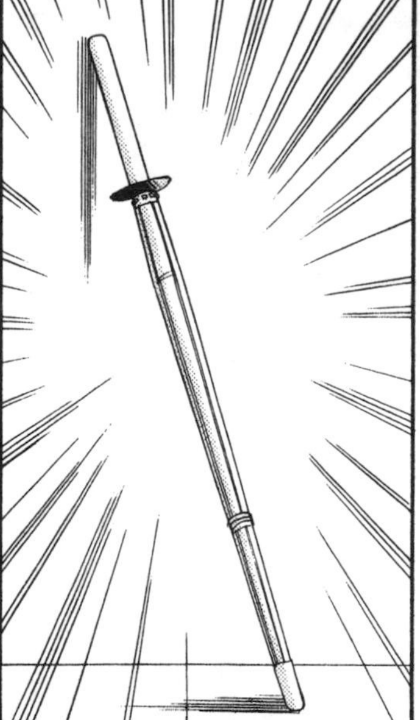

せんぱい
こぜう
YES, SIR...

バッ
BA (SNATCH)
10000 YEN

ダダダ
DADADA (DM DM DM)
ガタン
GATAN (SLAM)

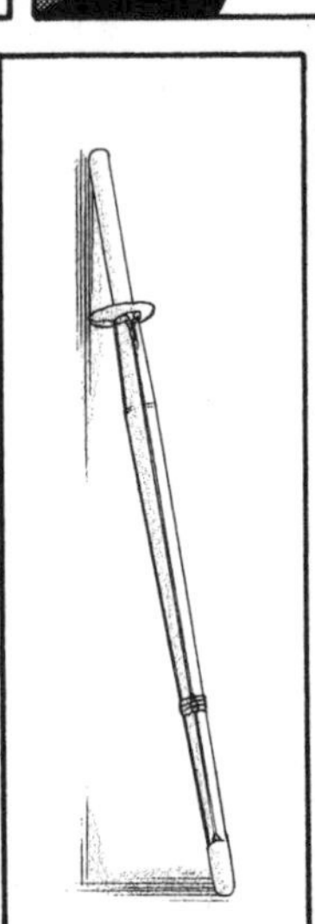

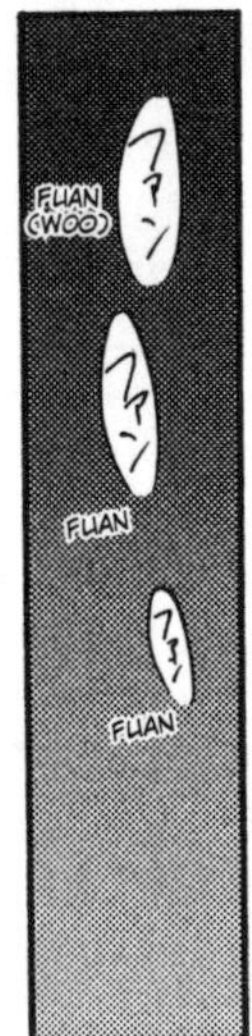
ファン
FUAN (WOO)
ファン
FUAN
ファン
FUAN

GA (SHKK)
DO (BOOM)
DO
DO
BUN (WHUMM)

ドッ
DO
(BOOM)

ドッ
DO

ドッ
DO

ドッ
DO

ドッ
DO

ドッ
DO

ドッ
DO

ドッ
DO

ALL RIGHT, TAMA!! ONE MORE TIME!!

JAS

CHAPTER 10
KOJIRO AND BENTO

WHERE ARE YOU GOING, KIRINO?

LET'S EAT LUNCH, ALREADY.

I'M EATING LUNCH WITH THE CLUB TODAY!

SORRY!

DO
(BOOM)

YES?

THAT'S, UH, A VERY MANLY LUNCH, TAMA-CHAN.
JUST A PICKLED PLUM AND RICE...
THAT'S COOL!

W-WELL, WE CAN ALL SHARE, I'M SURE.
HERE! THIS ISN'T ALL FOR DAN-KUN.

YOU HAVE QUITE A FEAST HERE.
YOU BET!
MY FAMILY RUNS A BENTO SHOP, ACTUALLY!
DID YOU MAKE THAT YOURSELF, MIYA-MIYA?
I SURE DID. OPEN WIDE!
UM, SORRY... I CAN'T SHARE MY PLUM.
W-WE KNOW! NOBODY WILL TAKE IT!
IT'S THE ONLY ONE YOU'VE GOT!
...
DOES ANYONE WANT MY RICE?
HUH?
UM, YEAH. OKAY, I GUESS...

I'M ALL DONE.
THAT WAS FAST!
YOU EAT LIKE A CHAMP, GIRL!

HERE, TAMA-CHAN! TRY MY HAM-BURGER STEAK.

もぐもぐ
MOGU (MUNCH) MOGU

HERE, TAMA-CHAN! MIYA-MIYA'S FRIED SHRIMP IS REALLY GOOD!

もぐもぐ
MOGU MOGU

DON'T FOR-GET TO WASH IT DOWN.

くぴくぴ
KUPI (GLUG) KUPI

I FEEL LIKE YOU'RE ALL FEEDING ME. YOU DON'T HAVE TO.
Y-YOU THINK SO?

YOU'RE JUST SO SMALL, IT MAKES US WANT TO FEED YOU TO MAKE SURE YOU GROW UP BIG!
I'LL GET FAT...
LABEL: MUROE

I GUESS WE STILL HAVE ONE MORE MEMBER, DON'T WE?

YEAH, HER NAME'S SAYA.
SHE'S A SECOND-YEAR, LIKE ME. WE'VE BEEN TOGETHER EVER SINCE WE STARTED GOING TO SCHOOL.
LABEL: PUDDING

WHY DOESN'T SHE SHOW UP?
UMM, WELL ...

THIS KIND OF STUFF HAPPENS, WITH HER.
HA-HA-HA-HA! LET'S JUST BE PATIENT WITH HER! TIME SOLVES ALL PROB-LEMS, YOU KNOW!
HA-HA-HA- HA-HA-HA-HA-HA-HA
...?

BUT WE'VE GOT THAT MEET COMING UP.
WE NEED HER TO COME SOON... WE'RE SHORT ON MEMBERS AS IT IS.
SUSHI! SUSHI!

SO WHAT WAS THE KENDO CLUB LIKE LAST YEAR?
WHAT WERE THE MEET RE-CORDS?

PRETTY NORMAL. WE'D BE EXCITED JUST TO WIN TWO IN A BEST-OF-FIVE TEAM MATCH.
LOOK WHAT OUR SUPER-VISOR IS.
THAT
SO, PRETTY NORMAL FOR BOYS AND GIRLS.

IN INDIVIDUAL MEETS, SOMETIMES ONE OF THE BOYS WOULD GET TO THE SEMIFINALS OR SO.
NOTHIN' DOIN' FOR THE GIRLS SINCE WE HAD SO FEW.
YEP YEP

STUDENT SPORTS REALLY DEPEND ON THE GUIDANCE OF THE SUPER-VISOR, AFTER ALL.
THAT
YEP, HE'S NOT TOO BRIGHT.

I REALLY LIKE THAT HE'S GOTTEN INTERESTED ALL OF A SUDDEN, THOUGH!
I CAN'T TELL HER WHY...
るんっ
RUN (WHEE)
SUSHI! SUSHI!

HOW WAS MIDDLE SCHOOL FOR YOU, YUJI?
YEAH! WERE YOU GOOD, YUJI-KUN?
HUH? ME?

I DUNNO IF I'D SAY I WAS THAT GOOD ...
MY BEST SCORE WOULD BE... MAYBE THE EIGHTH BEST IN THE PREFECTURE?
中田
LABEL: NAKATA

YOU MADE IT TO THE PREFECTURE QUARTERFINALS!?
THAT'S AWESOME!
NO, NOT REALLY! NOT AWESOME AT ALL.

NOT AWESOME AT ALL?
I SEE...

I NEVER EVEN GOT INTO THE PREFECTURE TOURNEY.
I'D LOSE AT THE LOCAL PRELIMS.
IF YOU'RE NOT AWESOME, I MUST BE NO BETTER THAN A SEA SLUG.
ねとー
NETOO (SLURRM)
WHAT? NO WAY, THAT'S NOT TRUE!
I'M AWESOME, I AM!
I'M TOTALLY THE BEST!!

I'VE BEEN DOING KENDO SINCE ELEMENTARY SCHOOL...
I WENT TO TAMA-CHAN'S DOJO.

DO YOU HAVE ANY OFFICIAL RESULTS, TAMA-CHAN?
I'VE NEVER BEEN IN A TOURNAMENT, SO NO...

WHAT A WASTE!
YOU COULD DO REALLY WELL IN A MEET, TAMA-CHAN!

...I COULD?
I CAN TELL HOW YOU'D DO, WHETHER YOU COMPETED OR NOT.

YOU'D WIN THE NATIONAL CHAMPIONSHIP!

ポリポリ
PORI (SCRATCH) PORI

HMM?

WELL, INVITE ME NEXT TIME!

LABEL: PRIVATE RICE

LABEL: EVERYDAY BREAD - SANDWICH SLICES

ALL RIGHT, PEO-PLE!!

THE PRACTICE MEET IS SOON!! WE'LL START PRACTIC-ING AT LUNCH BREAK TOO!!
ONCE YOU'VE FINISHED EATING, GET READY TO TRAIN!!

I'VE DECIDED THAT WE'LL ALL EAT HERE TO GIVE US MORE TIME!!
I WILL BE JOINING YOU MYSELF !!

MAKE SURE YOU ALL BRING BENTO LUNCH-ES!!
WOW, I CAN SEE WHAT YOU'RE AFTER.

NOW, MOVING ALONG ...
I'M GOING TO ORDER SOME PROTEC-TIVE GUARDS TODAY.
IT'S ACTUALLY A LITTLE EARLY FOR OUR BEGIN-NING MEMBERS TO BE WEARING THEM...
BUT I'VE GOT TO HAVE MIYA-MIYA PARTICI-PATE IN THE MEET, SO WE'VE GOT NO CHOICE.

坂口剣道具店
坂口剣道具店
剣道

SIGNS: SAKAGUCHI KENDO SUPPLIES / KENDO

モグ
MOGU (MUNCH)
剣道ガイドブック

MMM! DELI-CIOUS!!

SIGN: KENDO GUIDEBOOK

THE PERFECTLY-BALANCED SWEETNESS OF THE SWEET BEAN JAM, MADE LOV-INGLY FROM THE FINEST HOKKAIDO RED BEANS!
SURROUNDED BY THE THIN, SOFT RICE CAKE THAT MELTS IN YOUR MOUTH!
THIS LIGHT SALTINESS FOUND HIDING IN THE MIDST OF GRACEFUL SWEETNESS ORCHESTRATES A GLORIOUS MELODY OF...

ガラッ
GARA (SHHNK)

SIGN: PROSPERITY

ARMOR: SAKAGUCHI

YOU SHOULD HAVE SEEN HIS FACE WHEN HE LEFT.
...IT WAS THE HAPPIEST SMILE I'VE EVER SEEN IN MY LIFE...

AND WHO WERE THE MEMBERS MAD AT AFTERWARD? NOT HIM! NO! IT WAS ME!! WHAT'S THAT ABOUT!!?
WHEN SHOULD I SHOW UP?

HUH? OH NO, NO, NO! I COULDN'T TROUBLE A BUSY MAN...
OH, PLEASE! I WISH I WAS BUSY! I'VE GOT ALL THE TIME IN THE WORLD!

PLUS, IT'LL BE GOOD FOR YOUR CLUB TO BE TRAINED BY AS STRONG A TEACHER AS POS-SIBLE!
がっはっはっ
GA-HA-HA
カチーン
KACHIIIN (SNAP)

I KNOW YOU WERE ACTIVE BEFORE, BUT NOT FOR A WHILE.
BUT I STILL STOP BY THE DOJO ONCE A WEEK!

IF YOU WANT RESULTS, YOU SHOULD USE ME AS AN IN-STRUCT—
GOOD AFTER-NOON, SAKA-GUCHI-SAN.

ZAN
(ZSSH)

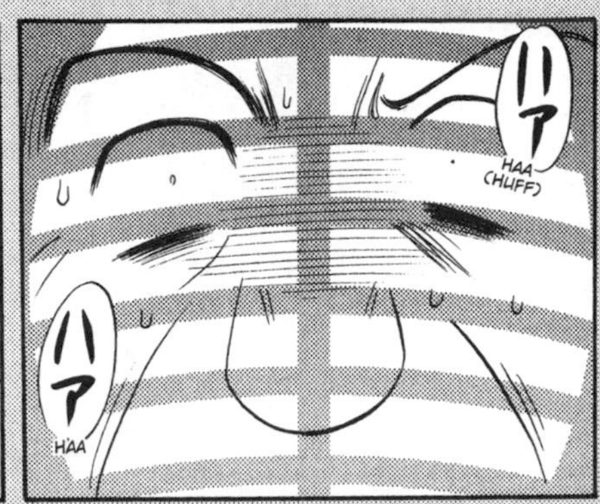

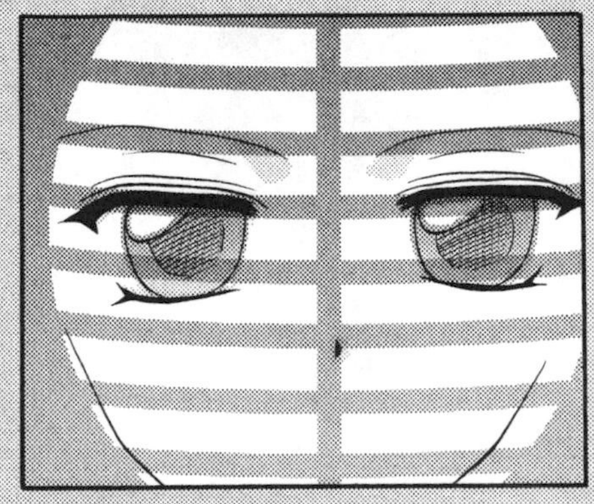

ARMOR: SAKAGUCHI

ARMOR: KAWAZOE

T...TAMA-CHAN!?

Y-YOU'RE ON THE TEAM? H-HOW ABOUT THAT!
THANKS FOR THE SPARRING, AS ALWAYS!
SAY HI TO YOUR FATHER FOR ME!

THE EX-PERIENCED MEMBERS ARE FREE TO BROWSE.
EIGA AND MIYA-MIYA, WE'LL START WITH SHINAIS.

I WAS THINKING I SHOULD GET A SABU-HACHI, MYSELF.

WHO'S "SABU-HACHI," YUJI?
YESSIR, M'LORD!
POTENTIAL SABUHACHI
NO, NO, IT'S JUST A TYPE OF SHINAI.

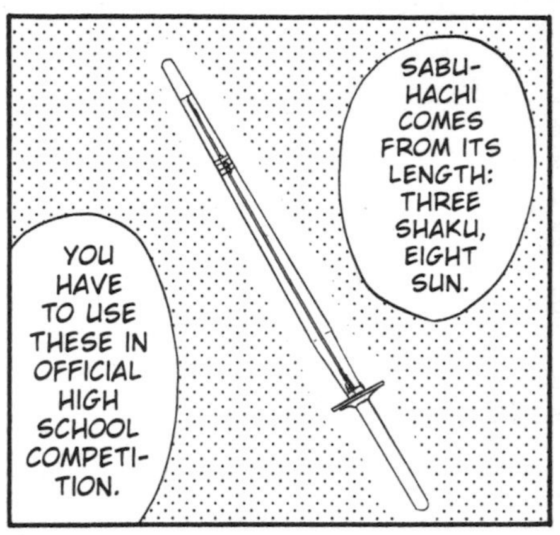
SABU-HACHI COMES FROM ITS LENGTH: THREE SHAKU, EIGHT SUN.
YOU HAVE TO USE THESE IN OFFICIAL HIGH SCHOOL COMPETI-TION.

THEY'RE ALL AROUND THE SAME LENGTH, BUT THE WEIGHT CAN VARY CONSIDER-ABLY.
THAT'S WHY YOU HAVE TO PICK UP EACH ONE TO GET A FEEL FOR IT.

AND NOT JUST HOLD IT, YOU NEED TO SWING IT.
IT MIGHT TURN OUT TOO LIGHT OR TOO HEAVY AT THE TIP.

WOW-WEE! SWEET BEAN TREATS!
もぐもぐ
MOGU (MUNCH) MOGU
I'M EX-PLAINING THIS FOR YOU!!

ZO
(SHIVER)

HUH?

...
NOTHING. NOTHING AT ALL.

OKAY, LET'S TRY ON THIS TORSO GUARD.

THESE AREN'T REALLY TOO DIFFERENT FROM SET TO SET, BUT TRY THEM ON ANYWAY!
I SUPPOSE THE GIRLS MIGHT WANT TO MAKE SURE THEY HAVE EXTRA ROOM AT THE CHEST.

SIGN: DELUXE EDITION

I WANT THIS ONE! IT LOOKS WAY COOLER!
HEY! THAT'S EXPENSIVE!!
DON'T PUT FINGERPRINTS ON IT!
BAN (BAM) BAN

KAPO (PLOP)

SIGNS: SAKAGUCHI KENDO SUPPLIES / KENDO

WHEEE! HOW DO I LOOK, MIYA-MIYA?
HE LOOKS SO LAME WITH IT OVER HIS UNIFORM...

わい わい
WAI (WHEE) WAI

MY SWEET BEAN BUNS ARE GONE!!

WELL, I'LL HAVE ALL OF THESE DELIVERED TO THE SCHOOL EARLY NEXT WEEK.
THANKS FOR ACCOMMODATING!

THOSE BUNS WERE REALLY YUMMY.
YES.
PERSONALLY, I PREFER WHEN THE RICE CAKE IS A LITTLE THICKER ON THE OUTSIDE.
TEKU (TROMP) TEKU

BUT AT THIS POINT, NO ONE COULD HAVE FORESEEN THE TRAGEDY THAT AWAITED WHEN THEIR GOODS WERE DELIVERED THE FOLLOWING WEEK...

TRANSLATION NOTES

Page 12
No-shows: As in America, Japanese schools have a variety of extracurricular clubs in different fields: sports, hobbies, crafts, etc. Depending on the school, it might even be mandatory that every student has joined a club, in which case you might have no-shows, or *yurei* ("ghost") members, who register for a club and then never show up to any after-school activities.

Page 15
Yakitori: Grilled chicken skewers. Very popular!

Page 23
Shinai: The name for the bamboo swords which are used in kendo.

Samurai movie: A common cliché of samurai-era period stories is the "trial by fire" to test a potential ally's ability as a warrior, usually by conducting a surprise attack to see if they respond adequately — if they can't handle it, they're probably not fit to fight alongside you!

Page 35
Leftover Bread Man: In Japanese, the students are calling him *Zanpanman*, meaning "Leftover Bread Man." This is a pun on the iconic children's manga/anime character, *Anpanman* (Sweet Bean Bread Man). One of the trademarks of the *Anpanman* series is a wide variety of bread-based characters following the same naming schematic, thus making it easy to invent nicknames such as this one.

Page 49
Comedy in Japan: Japanese people like to laugh just like everyone else, but their comedy comes in its own style. Rather than stand-up comedians who tell jokes and stories all by themselves, the most popular comedy format in Japan is the *manzai* duo, with a straight man (*tsukkomi*) and an off-the-wall man (*boke*). The *boke* role invokes goofy humor and the *tsukkomi* exists simply to point out the boke's mistakes, usually with a good slap on the head or the chest. If you've seen or read an anime/manga with a slapstick element, where one character is usually animatedly screaming at the others to shape up, you're witnessing the *manzai* dynamic at work. In this particular scene, you can hear the guys on TV delivering typical, non-descript *tsukkomi* interjections.

Page 76
Shoryuki: The name of this kendo meet (which exists only in the world of ***Bamboo Blade***) is a take-off on a real high school tournament that takes place in Fukuoka Prefecture called the Gyokuryuki High School Kendo Meet.

Page 119
Hakama: A long traditional skirt that is worn in many forms of Japanese martial arts including kendo, judo, and aikido.

Page 159
Shiso: The Japanese term for the perilla herb. Used in a variety of dishes for flavor, and has — as the story explains — anti-inflammatory properties that helps combat allergies.

Page 200
Bento: A traditional Japanese boxed lunch, which usually contains a portion of rice and several sides. There are many places to buy these in the morning for office workers short on time, but naturally, the best kinds are homemade!

Page 209
Koshihikari: The most common variety of rice grown in Japan. The "private" sack is a special kind given to rice farmers for holding rice they intend to keep themselves, rather than sell.

Page 217
Shaku/Sun: Archaic units of measurement. A *shaku* is roughly one foot (30.3 cm, precisely), while a *sun* is one-tenth of a *shaku*. They are only used in modern times to describe the length of swords and other traditional weapons. "Sabuhachi" comes from a combination of the numbers three (*san*) and eight (*hachi*).

ABOUT THIS MANGA - MASAHIRO TOTSUKA

BAMBOO BLADE IS THE FIRST MANGA WHICH I HAVE BEEN IN CHARGE OF AS A WRITER RATHER THAN AS AN ARTIST. MY JOB IS TO CREATE THE FOUNDATION OF THE MANGA IN THE FORM OF WHAT THE JAPANESE CALL A "NAME." THE "NAME" IS JUST A QUICK, SKETCHED-OUT STORYBOARD SHOWING THE PANEL STRUCTURE, PERSPECTIVES AND FACIAL EXPRESSIONS IN THE SIMPLEST WAY POSSIBLE. SOMETIMES I DESIGN THE CHARACTERS, AND SOMETIMES I DON'T. I'VE HAD IGARASHI-SENSEI CREATE SOME OF THEM FOR ME. WHY AM I JUST THE WRITER AND NOT THE ARTIST TOO? WELL, TO BE HONEST, IT'S JUST TOO MUCH WORK FOR ME TO HANDLE. SORRY! HOWEVER, I THINK IT'S CLEARLY FOR THE BEST THAT IGARASHI-SENSEI IS PROVIDING THE ART. OUT OF ALL THE STORY IDEAS I'VE BEEN SAVING UP, THIS IS CLEARLY MOST SUITED FOR SOMEONE WHO CAN DRAW GIRLS NICELY!

AT ANY RATE, I DIDN'T HAVE A LOT OF EXTRA WIGGLE ROOM IN MY SCHEDULE, SO I FIGURED THIS WOULDN'T BE MUCH LIKE MY OTHER SERIES, *MATERIAL PUZZLE*, WHICH HAD A TON OF DIFFERENT EXPANDING ELEMENTS IN THE STORY.

I NEVER MAKE NOTEBOOKS TO FILL WITH IDEAS; I PREFER TO JUST LET THINGS FLOAT AROUND INSIDE MY HEAD. I DIDN'T WANT TO GET THINGS TOO COMPLICATED, SO I DECIDED JUST TO MAKE MY CHARACTERS AND LET THEM LIVE AND EVOLVE WITHIN THEIR NORMAL, EVERYDAY LIVES. IT MAKES THINGS A LOT SIMPLER!

MY ORIGINAL INTENTION WAS TO MAKE A NICE, CONCISE STORY THAT I COULD END QUICKLY. THERE WAS MAYBE 3 TO 5 VOLUMES' WORTH OF MATERIAL ORIGINALLY, BUT SINCE THE STORY KIND OF TOOK OFF, I THINK IT WILL LAST LONGER. I'LL CONTINUE AS LONG AS I CAN, GIVEN MY HEALTH, SO I HOPE YOU'LL SHARE YOUR TIME WITH ME. THANKS, EVERYONE.

BACKSTAGE AFTERWORD
DRAWN BY IGARASHI
GOOD DAY, AND NICE TO MEET YOU.
GREETINGS!
I'M AGURI IGARASHI, THE ARTIST OF THIS MANGA. AS A SIDE NOTE, THE ONLY ASSISTANT I HAVE IS MY OWN DAD, WHO'S A TOTAL AMATEUR AT THIS STUFF.
I'M LOVING MY JOB HERE SINCE I WAS ENOUGH OF A FAN OF TOTSUKA-SENSEI'S MANGA THAT I HAD IT ON MY SHELF BEFORE THIS STORY EVEN GOT STARTED!
WELCOME TO MY BACK-STAGE STORIES!
BACKSTAGE NUMBER [1] TAMAKI-SAN
WE'VE GOT SOME EXTRA SPACE IN THE VOLUME. DRAW AN OMAKE!
打ち合わせ中。
STAFF MEETING
PHONE
UMM...
AN OMAKE?
YEP!
ANY IDEAS?
OKAY, THEN, WHY DON'T WE SHOW OFF TAMAKI'S ORIGINAL DESIGN!
NOTE: THE "E" STANDS FOR "EDITOR" HERE
WHAT WAS IT LIKE, AGAIN?
HA HA HA HA
SHE'S LIKE A DIFFERENT PERSON ENTIRELY! DON'T YOU REMEMBER? I LOOKED AT TOTSUKA-SENSEI'S CHARACTER CHART AND SOMEHOW GOT MY HEAD TURNED AROUND 180 DEGREES AND THOUGHT HE WANTED TAMAKI TO BE A TALL, GLAMOROUS, BABE! IF YOU SAW HER NOW, YOU'D BE LIKE, "WHO'S THAT!?"
OH, RIGHT! I RE-MEMBER NOW.
HA HA HA
TOTSUKA-SENSEI'S ORIGINAL TAMAKI DESIGN
YOU STILL GOT IT, THEN?
HEH HEH HEH!
YOU BET I DO!
SURE THING!
RIGHT HERE, IN FACT ...

い DOG ぬ

THIS IS A DOG!!
DON'T YELL AT ME!
E
PHONE

GETTING BACK TO BUSINESS.
FIRST SKETCH VERSION
TAMAKI (1)
HMM, MAYBE THIS COULD USE SOME MORE FEMININITY?
DOOOOON (BOOOOOM)
どーーん!
THIS IS MY ORIGINAL SUBMISSION SKETCH FOR TAMAKI (IS THAT REALLY TAMAKI?)

がっふ!
GAFFU (GLARF)

HAHA HAHA HA...
MAYBE WE SHOULDN'T DO THIS.
WHY NOT?
IT SUCKS.
DO IT!
IT SUCKS.

THIS IS GENERALLY HOW WE DO THINGS. HOPE YOU LIKE IT!

STAFF

STORY - TOTSUKA-SENSEI
ART - IGARASHI
HELP - DAD

SORRY FOR EXPOSING THIS DIRTY LAUNDRY, TOTSUKA-SENSEI.

VISIT AGURI IGARASHI ON THE WEB (JAPANESE ONLY) "ANTIHEROINE NEWS" HTTP://ANTIHEROINE.COOL.NE.JP/

BAMBOO BLADE ①

MASAHIRO TOTSUKA
AGURI IGARASHI

Translation: Stephen Paul

Lettering: Logan Johnson

BAMBOO BLADE Vol. 1 © 2005 Masahiro Totsuka, Aguri Igarashi / SQUARE ENIX. All rights reserved. First published in Japan in 2005 by SQUARE ENIX CO., LTD. English translation rights arranged with SQUARE ENIX CO., LTD. and Hachette Book Group through Tuttle-Mori Agency, Inc.

Translation © 2009 by SQUARE ENIX CO., LTD.

All rights reserved. Except as permitted under the U.S. Copyright Act of 1976, no part of this publication may be reproduced, distributed, or transmitted in any form or by any means, or stored in a database or retrieval system, without the prior written permission of the publisher.

The characters and events in this book are fictitious. Any similarity to real persons, living or dead, is coincidental and not intended by the author.

Yen Press
Hachette Book Group
237 Park Avenue, New York, NY 10017

Visit our Web sites at www.HachetteBookGroup.com and www.YenPress.com.

Yen Press is an imprint of Hachette Book Group, Inc. The Yen Press name and logo are trademarks of Hachette Book Group, Inc.

First Yen Press Edition: May 2009

ISBN: 978-0-7595-3005-8

10 9 8 7 6 5 4 3 2 1

BVG

Printed in the United States of America

AT ANY RATE, I DIDN'T HAVE A LOT OF EXTRA WIGGLE ROOM IN MY SCHEDULE, SO I FIGURED THIS WOULDN'T BE MUCH LIKE MY OTHER SERIES, *MATERIAL PUZZLE*, WHICH HAD A TON OF DIFFERENT EXPANDING ELEMENTS IN THE STORY.

I NEVER MAKE NOTEBOOKS TO FILL WITH IDEAS; I PREFER TO JUST LET THINGS FLOAT AROUND INSIDE MY HEAD. I DIDN'T WANT TO GET THINGS TOO COMPLICATED, SO I DECIDED JUST TO MAKE MY CHARACTERS AND LET THEM LIVE AND EVOLVE WITHIN THEIR NORMAL, EVERYDAY LIVES. IT MAKES THINGS A LOT SIMPLER!

MY ORIGINAL INTENTION WAS TO MAKE A NICE, CONCISE STORY THAT I COULD END QUICKLY. THERE WAS MAYBE 3 TO 5 VOLUMES' WORTH OF MATERIAL ORIGINALLY, BUT SINCE THE STORY KIND OF TOOK OFF, I THINK IT WILL LAST LONGER. I'LL CONTINUE AS LONG AS I CAN, GIVEN MY HEALTH, SO I HOPE YOU'LL SHARE YOUR TIME WITH ME. THANKS, EVERYONE.

BACKSTAGE AFTERWORD
DRAWN BY IGARASHI
GREETINGS!
GOOD DAY, AND NICE TO MEET YOU.
I'M AGURI IGARASHI, THE ARTIST OF THIS MANGA. AS A SIDE NOTE, THE ONLY ASSISTANT I HAVE IS MY OWN DAD, WHO'S A TOTAL AMATEUR AT THIS STUFF.
I'M LOVING MY JOB HERE SINCE I WAS ENOUGH OF A FAN OF TOTSUKA-SENSEI'S MANGA THAT I HAD IT ON MY SHELF BEFORE THIS STORY EVEN GOT STARTED!
WELCOME TO MY BACK-STAGE STORIES!
BACKSTAGE NUMBER [1] TAMAKI-SAN
打ち合わせ中。
STAFF MEETING
WE'VE GOT SOME EXTRA SPACE IN THE VOLUME. DRAW AN OMAKE!
E
NOTE: THE "E" STANDS FOR "EDITOR" HERE
PHONE
UMM...
AN OMAKE?
YEP!
ANY IDEAS?
E
OKAY, THEN, WHY DON'T WE SHOW OFF TAMAKI'S ORIGINAL DESIGN!
WHAT WAS IT LIKE, AGAIN?
E
HA HA HA HA
SHE'S LIKE A DIFFERENT PERSON ENTIRELY! DON'T YOU REMEMBER? I LOOKED AT TOTSUKA-SENSEI'S CHARACTER CHART AND SOMEHOW GOT MY HEAD TURNED AROUND 180 DEGREES AND THOUGHT HE WANTED TAMAKI TO BE A TALL, GLAMOROUS, BABE! IF YOU SAW HER NOW, YOU'D BE LIKE, "WHO'S THAT!?"
OH, RIGHT! I RE-MEM-BER NOW.
E
HA HA HA
TOTSUKA-SENSEI'S ORIGINAL TAMAKI DESIGN
YOU STILL GOT IT, THEN?
E
HEH HEH HEH!
YOU BET I DO!
SURE THING!
RIGHT HERE, IN FACT ...